# LALAS

## THE BOLD AND ADVENTUROUS JOURNEY OF A GREEK DREAMER

by Harry Mourelatos

Bloomington, IN  Milton Keynes, UK

authorHOUSE®

*AuthorHouse™*
*1663 Liberty Drive, Suite 200*
*Bloomington, IN 47403*
*www.authorhouse.com*
*Phone: 1-800-839-8640*

*AuthorHouse™ UK Ltd.*
*500 Avebury Boulevard*
*Central Milton Keynes, MK9 2BE*
*www.authorhouse.co.uk*
*Phone: 08001974150*

*First published by AuthorHouse 3/12/2007*

*ISBN: 978-1-4259-7020-8 (sc)*

*Printed in the United States of America*
*Bloomington, Indiana*

*This book is printed on acid-free paper.*

# Steve:

That very special day you came to me; a bundle of JOY!

And brought to me an immeasurable amount of GLORY!

I borrowed from the Sun, warmth, energy and STRENGTH

and promised to be offering you happiness until my last trace

of BREATH!

But, alas, the demons of this new world have now put

everything on HOLD.

They led you to fields so strange to you, to worlds which are so

ugly and COLD.

Sadly though, the link that has kept our thoughts TOGETHER

somehow broke up into pieces; it won't work now

maybe even NEVER.

One dark and tragic day you lost faith and trust in all of us who

loved you MOST.

You took a direction which, we, with pain in our souls, agreed,

 that it was the WORST.

Now that you are in heaven, I hope you found peace in the place

we mortals have never SEEN.

But I am always close to you, and I constantly feel your gentle

caress on my wrinkled SKIN.

# Acknowledgments

I wish to express my gratitude to my loving wife Marta Alicia and to our good friend Carolyn Karlin for their great help editing this book, and also my thanks to our good friend Jane Alcock for taking the photograph of my oil painting featured on the cover.

# CHAPTER 1 - My Beautiful youth

It is early in the morning; the sun just starting to show its golden rays over the mountain of Lykabettos and reflecting its bright color off the roofs of the houses as well as from the ancient buildings of this magnificent City of Athens, Greece. This is the capital city of the Country that has given the World the fundamentals for Civilization, Culture, Democratic Values, and rich History.

Moving out of the City to open spaces you are overwhelmed with the sweet aroma of beautiful flowers all over the place, namely yellow poppies, red tulips, chrysanthemums, jasmine, white and yellow margaritas, (those are the flowers which young lovers normally use to find the right answer by pulling its petals and asking, "You love me, you love me not"). But the flower of most abundance that covers miles and miles of open fields is the chamomile, which is very popular for its use in making tea.

In this place you hear the early birds singing their happy tunes; the cloud-free sky gives you that joyous feeling which makes you want to sing along with those happy birds. But you know there is a special reason for this natural offer of beauty. It is now the month of May; yes, this is the month I was born in this incredible City. It was the first of May of 1926.

May is the month of choice to visit Greece. It is the time of the year when everything comes to life. The Greek people have an incredible thirst for life and excitement, and after having gone through a typical wet winter, they are now ready to throw themselves into the most beautiful climate on the face of the earth. Now starts the season when they will work during the morning, go home for lunch, take a nap, and go back to work. But, after work they go out, yes out, and for hours and hours they walk around the streets, the parks, go to the open-sky movie theaters, just enjoying that gorgeous spring climate, or going to their favorite entertainment: DANCING, and so on, until autumn starts.

A few months after my birth my family, being of Greek Orthodox religion, brought me to this little, charming, and white stucco Chapel with worn out white marble stairs to baptize me.

Several years later my family and I went by that same Chapel, which is located in the small town of Falyron, about 15 miles west of Athens and just a few yards from the beach, surrounded by very old pine trees, which were bending backwards due to many years of attacks from those powerful winds coming from the storming Mediterranean waters.

There I was told the story of my Greek Orthodox baptism: I was taken into the Chapel, surrounded by family and friends. I was dressed in a white outfit, while crying my head off. Somebody took all my clothes off and then I was put into a big brass basin filled with warm water. The priest poured oil over my head and gave me the name of Haralambos, (later on I was given the nickname Lalas). Saint Haralambos is the patron and protector of Greek fishermen. I was wrapped in a white blanket and as per the Greek tradition, presented to my Godfather Panayioty Iconomou. Besides my parents, my Godfather was instrumental in shaping my entire professional career.

Thinking back about my life I have to admit that, due to my personality, my poor father had a special project in his hands to raise me. He had to walk on a tight rope dealing with me; on one hand, allowing me to exercise my free spirited, wandering, restless and independent personality, and on the other hand, developing basic discipline principles in me. That was not so an easy task for him. He was a very warm, loving, caring man, but he had an unusual background. First of all, he came from a large and successful family. My grandmother, Nina, who died in her sleep at a ripe age of ninety two, had twenty four pregnancies. Twelve survived, and nine of them lived on, my father being the oldest. When the First World War started my father ended up in the military, where he received a disability discharge. He then served as sheriff in a small village outside Athens for ten years and then retired from it. Discipline was a part of him, but he had to deal with my adventurous, curious, mischievous and wandering nature. I'll always remember many occasions from early stages of my life.

Here are some details of what I am trying to say. When I was about six years old, while playing with matches I started a fire in the kitchen. My father thought the best way to show me how dangerous it is to play with fire tied me to the railing of the bed for a few minutes to punish me and teach me, so that I would never play with matches again.

Some time later, we were living in an old three-story apartment, with a small courtyard, and a very narrow metal stairway. That day some strange commotion started to develop around our neighborhood. It turned out, that one older man from the third floor had just died. Since there were no other ways to put him in a casket and bring him down the narrow spiral type stairway they had to put him in a bag and drop him down with ropes. My parents considered this would be a very dramatic experience for me to see, so they sent me to the back bedroom. Sure enough, I managed to sneak out and went to the kitchen window and watched the whole process.

Some time later I remember going to school, being a few minutes late. As I reached the school building, I noticed that the class window was wide open. I stopped there a few seconds and I heard the teacher calling the names of the students. When the name Mourelatos was announced, I yelled with a loud voice: "HERE", and went to the classroom. The moment I walked in, the whole class started to laugh; the teacher, understandably, was furious. He grabbed me by my ear, took me in front of the class, and announced in a loud and sarcastic voice: "Look here boys and girls; we have a comedian in our class". But the most humiliating thing after my ordeal was when I was told by the teacher that in order to be admitted back in the classroom, my mother must come to school with me the next day, sit in front of the class, facing everybody, while I explain my dumb behavior.

Once there was a time when my mother and father were ready to go to a masquerade party. For some strange reason I didn't feel good about it, and I decided to do something to stop them from going out. A few minutes before they were about to leave I started pouting and complaining of stomach pains. My poor parents got so concerned; they called the family physician, who, after a careful examination, determined there were absolutely nothing wrong with me. Nevertheless, my parents missed the opportunity to enjoy a fabulous evening.

On another occasion, during school time, all the students were in front of the building singing the Greek national anthem followed by a prayer, which was a traditional ceremony. Instead of joining everybody, I decided to go upstairs to the class room. All windows were open, and while they were saying the prayer I felt it was my prerogative to start singing out loud, the national anthem. Just as I was about to finish, here comes this big tall school principal, fuming from both sides of his mouth, who grabbed me by my left arm and practically dragged me out the main school door. There I was, now on the top of those large stairs, facing a couple of hundred pupils, all of them laughing and making faces at me while the principal shouted at them: " This is a disgrace and I will not tolerate any one in this school doing what this pupil did." I remember going home, so humiliated, with tears in my eyes, hoping that my mother would understand that all I wanted to do was to entertain the whole school.

Since we are talking about mischievous activities, let us bring up one funny event. There we were, family and friends, in a place out in the country, having a good time, lots of food to eat and games to play. I always had my eyes on hard-boiled eggs. But this time my parents thought that I had eaten too many of them. So they put a bowl full of hard boiled eggs on this tall outdoor cabinet, (standing on uneven ground), and closed it but did not lock it. Now, while everybody was having a good time singing and dancing, I opened that cabinet, which, by the way, was loaded with plates, glasses, jars, and other foodstuff. As I reached for the bowl of eggs, I must have lost my footage and, as you can imagine, the whole cabinet started falling toward me forcing me to loose my balance. Then it started falling on top of me practically burying me. The screaming and yelling that took place from my parents and friends could be heard for miles and miles.

The interesting thing about all these mischievous behaviors of mine is that my poor father was always careful not to crush my enthusiasm while he would punish me. His routine way of punishment was to use his cane, (since he was disabled, he always carried a walking cane), so whenever, my brother, Rico, or I did something wrong which required punishment; my father's way of doing it was simple. "Go and bring me the cane," he would say, and the sooner we brought it to him, the softer the punishment. In spite of the objections from everybody who witnessed my father's routine, it seemed to work wonders. But, I must admit, what helped us the most while we were growing up was his love and affection for the whole family.

It is time now to move on to some more serious events that started to give me some sense of importance. I started to see the worldly events as they evolved around me, and made me feel there were people out there who mattered a lot. There were events which were taking place around and about me that I should try to pay attention to and attempt to comprehend even at that young age of mine.

It was now November the 3rd, 1935. In spite the fact that I was only nine years old, I began to grasp some of the political maneuvering taking place in Greece at that time.

Following a very liberal government headed by Eleftherios Venizelos, John Metaxas, then Prime Minister of Greece, fearing the growth of the Communist Party in Greece, closed down the parliament and established a fascist right-wing military dictatorship. Furthermore it was he, John Metaxas, who organized the return of George II, King of Hellenes, from exile and restored him to the throne that day.

It almost seems impossible, but I still remember that day. It was something read in history books. The anticipation, preparations, commotions, emotional upheavals, riots for and against the King. For my end of things, I was on the right side. My grandfather, Alexander, was a fanatical supporter of the King. Imagine this, in my grandparent's house if you open the door to the living room, you will be faced with a full size fancy poster of King Constantine the First, looking straight at you. As a matter of fact my grandfather and my father were regulars at the Palace. The way I heard it, King Constantine the First, who, after learning that my grandmother had so many pregnancies, presented her with a special cross. She wore it all the time. The cross started to lose its luster due to the perspirations from all those deliveries.

Now, going back to the day of the return of the King George II, all I remember was that our whole family got up early in the morning and walked to the main road, Singrou Avenue. Never in my young life had I ever seen so many, excited, loud, anxious people, all packed together by the side of the road, in about ten rows, hoping to be able to have at least a glimpse of the King. So there I was, squeezed from the right, squeezed from the left, trying to breathe fresh air, but all I was getting was a sour smell of perspiration and the smell of bodies which had not taken a bath, it seemed, for a whole month.

I was very intrigued by a double mirror square tube device that people on the back were using to be able to see what was happening in the front. Finally, after hours and hours of waiting, the procession started. An enormous amount of beautiful horses, which were carrying some handsome men dressed in colorful uniforms, wearing all kinds of medals and ribbons, and fancy hats that looked like the ones Napoleon used to wear, except, instead of wearing them sideways they were worn straight on. And, at the end, there came a huge carriage, with an open top, carrying the King and his wife Princess Elizabeth of Romania. It seemed as though everybody there was looking at something out of this world. They were screaming, crying, jumping up and down and acting as if they wanted to break the lines and rush to their side, and be even closer to them. I will always remember this as if it just happened yesterday.

Going back to my grandfather, trying to describe him, would need volumes. He was a man rather small in stature, with a sharp restless mind. He looked at you with those beady eyes, and a slight smile, revealing those stained teeth. While seated cross-legged, smoking his pipe, his legs shaking he would show his true personality: a deep thinker, a dreamer. He was a world traveler, deeply involved in the theatrical world, and boy, what a womanizer! His favorite expression was "Maria I can see your white ankle," when somehow a young lady's, long skirt (which was the style those days), happened to be raised up a bit, enough to show some white flesh.

But there he was, having to close down his theater in Alexandria Egypt, as well as the one in Athens, living in this huge home with my grandmother and a bunch of my uncles and aunts, in the old part of Athens.

The house was old and large with a long dark corridor and a dozen rooms. There was a huge living room, or "Salonie" as it was called, with a large oak table and beautiful armed chairs decorated with bright red velvet material. All the windows were covered with ceiling to floor red velvet curtains. There were lots of antiques, Persian carpets, mirrors, oriental vases and then some things which made the room look like something out of a palace. In that very room many guests would come for entertainment. The big table would be moved aside, the old gramophone would be cranked up, the music would start and everybody would start dancing. However, something strange always happened when masquerade parties would take place in the house; guests would arrive in regular clothes, then they would go to one of the rooms (where a bunch of trunks full of theatrical dresses were stored), and put on those beautiful dresses and colorful masks. Then the party started, and later on they went home, still wearing those theatrical attires. The same event was repeated so many times, until there were no more dresses left in the trunks. To him, all this was a continuation of his life's ambition, entertaining people.

And speaking of entertainment; that was built in our family's subconscious. When it came to partying, bed time for my sister, my brother and me was always without restrictions. Greek people like to teach children to dance before they learn how to walk. First they held you up while dancing, then as you are barely able to walk they would take your left hand to their right hand, your right hand to their left hand, then your left foot on their right foot and your right foot on their left foot, and they followed the music, and now you were dancing. As a matter of fact, it was our mother's love of music, which instilled in us the wonderful feeling for music. She would put as in bed at night, leave our bedroom door slightly open, and crank up that old gramophone, playing the old classics i.e. Mozart, Chopin, Liszt, etc. until we fell asleep.

Back now, to my grandparents. Money started to become a big concern, so they moved to a smaller two-story house just a few yards from the foot of the Acropolis. Fortunately for us, we were living about thirty minutes walking distance from them, so visiting them was our special treat. First of all, the location of their house was so unique. Basically, it was very close to the Herodes Atticus ancient theater of Dionysus! During the summer months, if all the windows were open, you could hear all the major performances played at that theater, such as the classic, Oedipus, Electra, Agamemnon etc., which was fabulous.

There was a totally different activity however, that I enjoyed the most while visiting my grandparents. The Acropolis was just walking distance from their house and it was an ideal place to climb those big boulders, and fly a kite there. To my amazement, while I was so concentrated in flying my kite, I was also disturbed by all those strange people, who were wearing all types of outfits, and speaking different languages. I had no idea what they were trying to say, looking so excited, pointing here and there, and taking pictures while stumbling over those rocks. But then, who was I to know. After all, this was the famous and historical Parthenon which was within their reach after they had traveled thousands of miles just to get a glimpse at it, and, here I was, kind of distracted by their presence, while I was trying to reach the heavens with my precious toy.

Now is the time of the year in which our family has been looking forward to for months. It is the beginning of summer. Now, as well as for many years to come, we would start our yearly preparations to move from our rented house to our seaside place by the Aegean Sea, which was named Kavouri. What an enjoyable expectation! The whole affair was the result of my father's idea to offer us the most pleasurable summers at the minimum cost. Because he was retired we were raised on a very small income; he would rent a house from October through the end of May, when school was over. Then our whole household would be packed-up, some items would be stored and the rest would be loaded to a wagon and we would be on our way to paradise, Kavouri.

At the beginning, all we had to live in was a huge tent. After that, we started living in a good size shed, which we all worked on to build, from the cement frame foundation to the tar roof. The following year, my uncles decided to build a good size cabin next to us. From then on, the whole Mourelatos clan would be together the entire summers. One can never imagine what a thrill it was for all of us to spend hours, days, and nights together in such a dream place.

Kavouri at that time was practically unknown. It is located about seventeen miles southwest of Athens. Its name comes from the fact that its aerial view is the shape of the crab (which in Greek means Kavouri). Arriving there you come down the hill from the main road and are faced with a breathtaking view of the Aegean Sea. You look at the incredible colors of the water, starting with clear color, which changes to green, to blue, to dark blue all the way to the end where the sky meets the ocean. Coming close to the beach you see those pine trees trying to reach out to the water while they are whispering their sleepy tune. But, before you are able to reach the water you must climb up and down those huge sand dunes which stand as a protective fort, so it would not be too easy for the intruders to spoil that magnificent sight.

Our life there was basically pure and simple. We would get up in the morning, put on our bathing suits, never wear shoes, and go up the hill to cut some wood for our mother to cook breakfast in a fireplace, which was made out of rocks and a couple of iron bars. After breakfast we cleaned up around the area and went to the beach until noon. We came home, had lunch, took a nap for a couple of hours, and then went back to the beach. We came back home around six o'clock to have dinner, and play games. Everybody would start to sing various songs, tell stories, and then go to bed, so we could start anew next day.

To describe here all that was happening during the hours we were spending at the beach would take volumes, so let as talk about the most pleasurable events of the average day.

Going to the beach would only take about five minutes. Right in front of us there was a small, charming island the size of a large house. We would be able to walk to it; the water level was never above the knee. On that island you could find all types of sea animals, i.e. fish (all kinds), crab, shrimp, octopus, jellyfish, sea urchin and more. We would do most of our fishing using nothing more than our bare hands. It was so easy, because there were so many small caves among the rocks that all we had to do was to kneel down in the shallow water, put both hands together and there you were holding a bunch of small shrimp, a crab or whatever. What I remember the most was that when we caught a shrimp, we put it in our mouths, still alive, moving it around our tongues for few moments, and finally we would chew it and swallow it. The one who kept them longest in their mouth was the winner!

Some of the rocks of that island were very good size, in fact they were like boulders and we used them to jump from them for diving competition.

There were some very fascinating activities that I must not forget to describe here. From time to time, we would hear various vendors coming by with their donkeys shouting, "Fresh watermelons," or "Fresh vegetables," or "Fresh fish, "or "Drinking water," or "Ice cream". Oh boy, that would create such excitement, especially the watermelons. My father insisted on buying the whole load from that guy, at a bargain price of course. It seemed as though there was a mountain of watermelons seated right next to our outdoor table. There were also many times, at early evenings, we would  go down to the beach to watch the fishermen pulling their fish lines and unloading their fish right in front of us, and they bargained for good prices with my father, so we had a really good meal for a few days to come.

The moonlight was always such a magnificent sight, that most of the friends of our family would try to take advantage of it and many times they will surprise us and just show up in the middle of the night, with their guitars, or violins, or harmonicas and we would all get up, go to the top of the hill and enjoy their serenades for hours.

Going back to some of the memories which were stuck in my mind in regards to my Grandfather, was his classical way of telling stories about his past life, the excitement of running his theater business. Having a glass of retsina, a Greek wine, as he was seated under a huge pine tree, smoking his pipe he would call me, "Hey Lalas, don't you see that my carafe is empty? Go down to the store and ask Yanis to fill it up". And there I was, in the darkness of the night, going down the hill, the ocean sounding its normal thundering noise, the white waves showing up their contrasting bright colors in the darkness of the night. I would walk into this primitive like hut, holding the empty carafe, and go to the corner of the room where this old rusted barrel was resting atop big rocks. I would put the carafe under the faucet, turn it on and I could hear, what always fascinated me, the sound of "clink, clink, clink," as the wine was pouring into the carafe. Going back home holding that "precious wine", I could just picture that gleaming expression on my Grandfather's face. He would chuckle his teeth; pour some wine in his glass and give out an exuberant "WOW", while looking at the glass as if it were a rare jewel.

Some of the most memorable times came along when one of my uncles bought a small sailing boat, about twelve feet long. It looked just like the ones you would find hanging on the side of rich yachts, made out of fine wood, pure white bottom, lacquered top and sides, with brass type hooks and brackets. We would spend hours and hours riding it, as well as cleaning it after each ride (just for the fun of it.)

We never had any dramatic experiences with it except one unforgettable time. It was one late afternoon, and one of my uncles and two of their friends decided to sail out in spite of the fact that stormy weather was brewing out there in the open sea, and, against the advice of family members, not to attempt such a trip. It turned out to be a total nightmare. The hours and hours of waiting to see them come back was followed by darkness. The rescue authorities were informed and arrived in a short time. The wind by now was at its fullest force, the waves seemed to have developed into very angry, huge, breakers, and the moon was covered with some ugly dark clouds which made the whole atmosphere look like out of a scary book. Our whole family, as well as many friends and curious bystanders, were there anxiously waiting for some positive outcome, but to no avail. Finally everybody, including the rescue authorities, with incredible disbelief on their faces, as to what had just happened, decided to go home. About four o'clock in the morning everybody started to hear voices coming from the beach which started to sound like a very exciting yelling, like "I see them, I see them, they are safe, and they are coming back". Before we knew what was happening, everybody got up; half dressed, and ran to the beach. There, as far as we could see, the silhouette of a tiny sail boat was in sight. It seemed like the prayers of everyone was heard. It felt as though it took forever for the boat to arrive at the beach, having to fight the strong opposing winds, which seemed to push that little boat, back to the deep waters. But they made it, and were treated like heroes! There they were, all three of them, looking haggard, and trying to hide the fact that they were exhausted and deliberately trying to cover their embarrassment for taking such a foolish chance. After they had a moment to rest, they started explaining some of the details of their ordeal.

This was basically what happened; as soon as they were about a mile out, the wind took control of the boat and the best they could do was to allow it to  sort of drift toward a deserted island, about ten miles out. They stayed there a few hours to gain some strength and then attempted to return to the beach, and after struggling and fighting the natural enemy, they made it back to tell us their story.

Now, turning the pages, so to speak, to a different life style. There were a few times that we had a chance to go to Kavouri during the wintertime. That had some different feeling though; we had to spend our time in my uncle's cabin because it was waterproof and warm. You could hear the powerful thunder of the water breakers threatening to force themselves through the windows. We would lie down in bed at night and our father would do his favorite thing reading all kinds of books to us, mostly mystery types; his preference being Sherlock

Holmes. But as I recall he would fall asleep and we would have to wait until the next day to finish the story.

Going back to our summer times, about the middle of October, my poor mother would travel to Athens and start scouting for a new place for us to move in and live during winter and spring, (during school season). What a sad experience for all of us. None of us liked the winters, but we knew, after all, that in few months we would be saying, Kavouri here we come!

Basically this was our lifestyle, until October 1940, when our exciting, fun way of living, and all those wonderful memories suddenly came to an abrupt END.

# CHAPTER 2 -
# The Horrors of War, German Occupation, and Communism

For months and months now the whole world is going through an enormous anxiety. Since Adolph Hitler rearmed Germany, in violation of Treaty of Versailles, he started to put to use his ambitious plan to conquer most of the world. By now he was able to occupy most of Europe. The Nazi Axis with the cooperation of Italian Fascists was planning to go through Greece in order to attack Africa. Every day now, at every moment, we were in a state of alert. The preparation for war was at its highest level. The state officials made sure we were totally prepared for war. Every household was stocking food, water, medical supplies, etc; the lights had to be covered with dark material and the windows had to be covered with black paper. The homes with basements were designated as shelters for the surrounding community and were open to the neighbors for their use. Schools were given specific instructions for possible closings and alternative uses. The subject of the day was: WAR! WHEN! What anybody would do or could do? Can we avoid it? Who can help us? Maybe with the assistance of the British we will be able to stop an invasion.

Finally, on October 28th, 1940, at 5:30 a.m., an ultimatum was delivered to Greece by the Italian Embassy in Athens. We were required to cede various coastal positions and strategically important islands to the Italians within three hours. General Metaxas, head of the Greek Council of State, refused those demands with his Historic, "OXI", meaning: "NO", in Greek. Within a few hours, on the same day, an Italian invasion into Greece (from the previously conquered Albania, by Italian troops) had begun.

That dreadful expectation of WAR was now upon us. The whole country was now in the state of shock. People gathered around at the stores, school centers, churches, on the streets, and were wondering what this is all about. During early evenings, people would find themselves rushing home, a very unusual behavior for a Greek, who normally enjoys the nightlife. The nights now revealed a surreal, spooky type of feeling, very dark, quiet and full of anxiety. The dark skies were all of a sadden covered with bright stripes of aerial searching lights and the defense sirens were now in full operation, which made everybody feel like any minute now the enemy airplanes would start bombing us.

The home our mother had selected that time happened to be somewhat elevated, about five steps, with a small basement in the rear of the house, about ten feet wide by twelve feet long. It qualified as a shelter for the immediate neighborhood.

I will never forget that particular night; about two o'clock in the morning the sirens went on and some of the air defense shooting started. My sister, Rena, was very frightened and asked my father "What are we to do now? Where are we going? "And his answer was, with a trembling voice; "We must go down to the basement, right now". So we rushed down the stairs, and to our amazement, there were a number of people already there, squeezed in the dark room, children complaining, babies crying, older folks coughing and moaning. Fortunately, it did not last more than a couple of hours, but it sure felt like a century long.

That kind of experience became almost routine; day in and day out, you go by your life not knowing what it would happen next.

The actual war, up in the Greek-Albanian borders was now in full force. The resilient Greek army had just surprised the whole world with their bravery. More and more news was received that the Greeks repelled the Italians and forced them back to the Albanian territories. We would hear on the radio, every day that we were winning the war. We were loosing many soldiers in the process however. Many of the wounded soldiers were transferred to various hospitals. Some of them near our home. One day my sister, Rena, suggested that we go and visit a local, large hospital, where a number of wounded soldiers had just arrived for treatment. She became so emotional when seeing those poor, young soldiers, with arms and legs missing, faces covered with white wrappings, blood all over them, that she started to cry. It did not take long, however, for her to get very close to one of wounded soldiers. If I remember correctly, his name was Panos. After several visits, we all realized that something was developing between my sister and Panos! It turned out that he had fallen in love with her to the extent that he asked to see my father. When my father and all of as visited Panos at the hospital, with tears in his eyes, he expressed his desire to talk to my father alone. What he really had to say surprised all of us. He had fallen in love with my sister and he wanted to ask for my father's permission to marry her. Of course that could never happen; Rena was not even seventeen years old. But how would any young man who laid eyes on her not fall in love with her? Her powerful, beautiful brown eyes, her slender gracious body, her pale soft skin, made her look irresistible. Poor Panos, he had to have some time to wait for his turn, if any, but this was something to remember.

Since the Italian forces were repelled back to the Albania territories, there were thousands and thousands of them captured as war prisoners and sent all the way back to camps very close to where we lived. We received a word one day that many prisoners would be arriving on foot in the area. So we went down to the main road, just to watch them. What a sad and painful experience it was. All those poor young men, looking haggard, weak, starving, cold, hardly being able to walk, made you feel so sorry for them and forget they were the enemy. But they were, and also losing the war.

Hitler and the Axis forces, disturbed by the turn of events, sent German forces into Greece to prop up the faltering Italians. That in itself was the major turn of events of the war against Greece. The enormous German military power was so overwhelming it didn't take long to overpower the relatively small Greek military forces. Things changed fast, and we started to feel that the inevitable was coming. Practically every night the sirens went on. We could hear the enemy planes roaring over our heads and some distant bombing, which made everyone fearful of what would come next.

We were now in the middle of the war. The ugly winter, the rain, the snow in northern Greece was at its fullest extent now. Our soldiers were killed, wounded, and suffering from frostbites so much that the whole population was now at full speed working hard to help anyway possible. Men, women, and children were devoting hours and hours learning how to knit all types of clothing for the military, mostly socks. Even I was taking lessons on how to knit socks and gloves. The word was going out on the radio, the newspapers, on the streets, or wherever, that our soldiers were loosing their legs, hands and their spirits, simply because they could not cope with the freezing conditions up the rough Greek mountains. That situation made a very bad impression on everybody. I remember my poor mother working frantically on socks, scarves and mittens, "Just to see if I can save some young man's life", she would cry out!

So, there we were, about six months into the war, which seemed like a lost cause. People were killed, wounded, and amputated. By now we were faced with food shortages, which started to cause the worst fear of all.

Then, before we knew it, the terrible news came out. Our forces were defeated, and the Greek army surrenders to the German forces. Within a few days the German tanks were rolling in the streets of Athens followed by thousands of German troops. The war was now ended, but the horrible German-Italian occupation had just started.

One can not understand the enormity of the change of life that occurs until one goes through that type of experience. You go about your new life wondering, "What is this all about? What is going to happen next? Am I no longer a free person? If I do something wrong, am I going to a prison camp? Or am I going to be executed?"

The immediate effect for us was the closing of our school. The German army closed the school and converted it to a military camp. So now we would go to classes held in the nearby park, seated on the ground trying very hard to concentrate on the lecture, but it had to be done. Later on we were able to move classes to a nearby Church; that was an improvement. It did not take time however, for us to realize that the situation would get a lot worse than we thought at the beginning. The shortage of all of life's necessities, such as food, supplies, energy, etc, started to have an effect on the whole community. Soon after the occupation started we had to wait in line to buy groceries, if we could find some, most importantly bread.

It didn't take long, however, for people to start suffering from lack of food. You could see in their faces the need for some nutrition. The government was not in a position to do anything about it. The German armies, with thousands of soldiers living here now, were using every conceivable supply for their own benefit. We were all starving. The choice at hand was food rationing. You could only qualify for a small amount of food. There was no flour available for us so we had to rely on corn bread. More and more people were now desperate for food. There were times that some could not make it home, and the next morning, on our way to school, we would find them dead on the street. I must say here that I can never forget that particular time when, while waiting in line for my corn bread ration (a mere handful), I saw a mother holding her two year old son, who was obviously starving; rush to a man who was holding his rationed portion, grab his bread and in desperation, stuff it to her son's mouth, as if it was her last hope to save him from a sure death.

There was another sad event that is very vivid in my mind. A young man in his teens, living in a basement just next to us, seemed as though he needed food badly. We tried to help as much as we could. His family was very poor. But no matter what, nothing seemed to help him; he started to look like a skeleton. Eventually he died from starvation and he had to be moved out in a wheelbarrow to be buried somewhere nearby. All that happened right in front or our bare eyes.

The only reason we managed to survive was because my father used his ingenuity to fool the Germans. Here it is how that happened.

My Godfather manufactured pine-gum products, which the Germans needed to make war products, so the Germans issued special permits for his trucks to go out of the city to various villages. My father would ride along on those trucks, and while they were out in the farms he would buy some bread, butter, cheese, etc, and hide them in the containers at the lower level. When the Germans stopped them at the check post, all they could to see were the containers of pine-gum products, so they let them through. Although that did not happen often, it helped us to have some food on the table and that was the reason we survived while thousands of other people around us starved to death.

By now we all realized that the occupation is here and going to be with us for a long, long time. Besides the obvious starvation some new fearful developments started to come about. Anti-occupation groups started to surface. They came under different codes and names. Some started killing German soldiers and of course the Germans would respond vigorously. The curfew started to limit our lives to a minimum. No person would be allowed on the streets without a permit after eight PM and until six AM. Although that seemed too restrictive, at the same time it gave us an opportunity to have more social activities. We would go to a party and spend the whole night dancing and playing games and having a good excuse not to come home at the regular time.

The resistance groups started to get more aggressive but so did the Germans. One day after two Germans were killed, we went downtown and saw hundreds of people kneeling in the middle of the town square for hours, surrounded by German soldiers. What a horrible sight! We heard the next day that three people were selected from that group, put against the wall and were executed, "as an example and a warning." But it was not clear to me that all Germans were that bad. For instance, just a few blocks from our house there was an open space, like a small park, in which the German army decided to use as a camping ground for a couple of hundred soldiers, protected with barbed wire, a gate and a number of guards stationed at various spots . That camp happened to be on our way to school, so, day after day as I was going by, I would see the same guard looking at me, and smiling and eventually he said something that sounded like ," Hello". After a while I would stop and say something to him in Greek, and to my amazement, he would reply in Greek, saying "How you are doing?" And so on and so on. That happened so many times that by now I felt free to ask more questions and I received incredible responses. First of all, he told me that his name was Hans, and that he had a son about my age; he expressed dislike for the war, and specifically the attack on Greece. I kept saying to myself, "This is a good person; how can he be an enemy?"

After talking to him for a while, I realized that I was dealing with a well educated person. One day he looked straight in my eyes and started to recite Homer's poetry, in perfect Ancient Greek. That made such an impression on me, that to this day, I can not erase it from my mind.

What a dilemma; there I was, a fifteen year old Greek boy trying to be friendly with the enemy, a German soldier! Seemed so awkward; I was not even supposed to be talking with Hans, but, on the other hand, he sounded so human. He started explaining to me that most Germans felt it was not right for them to be here. Greece, to him was the country which created the modern civilization and the foundation of Democracy, and it should not be destroyed. That was hard to believe coming from an enemy, but he was not, in my mind, in that category; he was different.

This friendship became more complicated as the months went by. As I said before, the anti-occupation movement started to evolve. Every time I met with friends, the subject of underground activities would be the main topic. Even if you didn't want to get involved, you would be, almost without a choice. Either you would go and do something or you were not a true Greek. I found myself in the same position that practically every one of my good friends was involved in, somehow. The most common thing was to meet at various places, in somebody's home for a "party". There, a "big shot" would start talking about a movement of some sort. "The enemy must not be without resistance, we must find ways to show that we are against the occupation," etc, etc. Our first assignment was to go out at night and paint out all kinds of graffiti, like "Germans get out of Greece", or "Death to Hitler" or

"Greeks need food", e.g. At first it seemed kind of scary, but after a while I got used to it. I remember that one night it was a very close call. A German patrol car came so close to spot us that we had to drop the buckets of black paint and run for our lives.

One day, something strange happened as Hans and I were talking. All of a sudden he started to lecture me, and with a strong voice he stated that, "It is dangerous and so stupid for some kids, to go out at night and write those things on the walls." He further said, "Those kids are looking for trouble and they could be killed on the spot." I started trembling, not knowing how to respond to that statement, so I sort of nodded like I kind of agreed with him. How he would feel if he knew that the night before I was one of those kids playing with fire, I thought to myself.

Things were by now getting harder, thousands of people were dying from starvation, food was scarce, the German army after having succeeded in conquering Europe, was moving towards Africa. The movement against occupation started to become a big issue. I found myself getting more and more involved as the months and years went by. I was feeling the pressure to do things that I was not too sure about. The group of people I was dealing with made me feel that they had some kind of agenda that was strange to me. The first time I realized that I was in something that had some outside influence was when, at this particular party, as I was enjoying my favorite activity, (dancing to American music), a strange looking character with a red cap and a beard, took me aside and started to lecture me about my choice of dancing, "We don't do this kind of dancing; we like Polka, and Russian music" he said, with some emphasis in his voice. That was the turning point for me. I was now suspicious that something not so good to my taste was going on and I started to ask questions, wondering what I was getting into.

After some time dealing with them I came to realize that the main drive behind some of those underground activities, was based on communistic influence. However, it was not clear to me to what extent the communists were controlling those movements. It turned out that there were about three types of movements, the conservative, the liberal, and the communist. For some reason I decided to lean toward the middle, and that was not a good choice. Before I knew it I was out at night more and more, passing flyers, painting graffiti, and all of a sudden I was given a rifle to, "prepare for the help of liberating Greece from the German occupation". I was now in too deep. I had no idea what to do with that rifle. I was given instructions on how to use it and I found open spaces to shoot targets, like bottles and cans. Fortunately those people sensed that their ideologies were not my kind of thing so they never trusted me enough to offer me any mission, and luckily, I never had a need to use that weapon. It turned out that I was misled; the group I was involved with, although not communist, the KKE as it was known, it was nevertheless influenced by communistic principles. That alone resulted in a lot of conflicts between those three different groups to the extent they started to fight amongst each other. What a mess! What originally started out to be a noble movement, an effort to liberate our country from the German occupation, turned out to be a fight of Greeks against Greeks, which was influenced from different ideologies and were basically brokered by communists.

By now the Germans started to lose the war. The Allies now had gained strength in Africa and Europe and with the help of British and Americans; Greece was now liberated from the Germans.

It was such an incredible experience! The streets were filled with British soldiers, who were parading around with their Scottish music, people running up and down the streets, laughing, singing, dancing, all the way past midnight. But the best part was that we now had food and there was more to come. After four years of a BRUTAL occupation, our turn to come back to normal life came very quickly. Thanks to President Truman and his Marshal Plan, Greece, along with many other European countries, received enormous financial help and started to move toward some degree of normality. But for me it was not that simple, because after the German army was moved out, my group was outlawed by the government. I had to flee my home and hide for a few months, taking refuge in the mountains outside of Athens along with a bunch of some strangers, moving by foot from one village to another, practically starving, until the government declared amnesty to all underground groups. I was then able to return home to my family, who were almost exhausted from fear and concern about what might have happened to me. But they were very relived and happy to see me back and well!

# CHAPTER 3 – A New Me

I was now a new person, a free person, free from the Germans, free from my stupid involvement with that group. I was beginning to think of my future, what did I like the most? Well, music was my first choice.

The love of music seemed to have been implanted on me from my mother. All the years I had known her I always remembered her entertaining others. Any time we would go and visit her sister Sofia, my mother would sit by that beautiful piano and start playing all kinds of songs, classics, pop, anything, all by ear, never having any formal training. I remember sitting next to her and looking at her fingers moving right and left and admiring what she was able to accomplish so effortlessly, and with such a satisfaction in her face! I was so impressed! Many times, we would go to various parties and she would take someone's guitar, stand up and play and sing with such warm expressions that everyone had tears in their eyes. All that was part of my mother's soul, it was a part, which indeed, matched her physical beauty, those powerful brown eyes, soft pale skin, all put together on a relatively tall statuesque body, (she was actually taller than my Dad). It seemed that those attributes of my mother's had a strong influence on me, maybe even more that I had originally realized.

One day my luck smiled at me. As I was walking down the street, I stopped to talk to a neighbor and I heard somebody inside the house, playing an accordion. So I asked her, "Who is playing?" She was nice enough to invite me in and introduce me to Mario. It turned out that Mario was an Italian soldier who had decided to defect and found refuge in their house. He had brought with him his accordion, and that was not all, Mario needed money and he had to sell it so he could find his way back to Italy. I saw that beautiful instrument; it was a full size accordion. When holding it while sitting on a chair it would be from my lap all the way to my chin. It had a black luster color and was decorated with bright red, green, yellow and white stones. I rushed back home to tell my parents how much I loved it and if there was any way we could afford it I would be so thrilled, although I did not have any hope because we were poor. But time was of essence; Mario had to move on fast, being afraid that he might be discovered. My good father had an idea. He called my Godfather and pleaded with him to help us finance it and that did it. I was now in heaven. That instrument turned my life around. I was so involved with the accordion nothing else mattered. I decided I need to get some lessons.

Luck was going my way. I found a teacher, a woman, who was so into accordions that she took me under her wings and tried to make me a "professional" accordion player, to the extent that, to my amazement, after a couple of months of training I found myself playing next to her in an open- air night club.

So, there I was, playing accordion for friends, in school, and for relatives. The most rewarding experience, as I recall, was, when sometimes during the warm nights, I would sit in our back porch, which was kind of elevated, and started playing, and all of a sudden I would see the neighbor's lights come on, one after another, obviously wanting to listen to my music. What a thrill! I started thinking ,where all that would lead to? Is there a future in this kind of adventure? I was not too sure I had an answer to that.

In the mean time I finished high school and was getting ready to go out and face the world.

Life around me started to be more enjoyable. After I graduated from high school my first priority was to start making some money. By some good luck and my father's connections, I found a good job working for the Greek Airlines as a ground service representative. Wow, what can I say except that I was on the top of the world! Not only did I make some fairly good money, I wore a nice uniform, met interesting people from all over the world, and for the first time in my life I got the feeling that Greece seemed to offer me limited opportunities. I saw all those people coming out of the airplanes from all over the world, especially America, and I started to realize that my desire to go to America some day and live the kind of life I had seen it in the movies, could become reality. But in order to accomplish that I had to find a way to finance it. The idea was getting to me more and more. I started paying more attention to what America was all about and I felt that it was the place I wanted to be, but how? I talked a lot about it to my mother and father. They were the kind of parents who would never do anything that stop us from moving ahead in life. My father, for some reason, made me believe that I had the intellect to be able to go to the University and become some sort of a professional. My Godfather thought that, since he was in the chemical business, I should think about becoming a chemist, and he was willing to finance my education. However, to be accepted to the University of Athens, in the Chemistry department, was an enormous task. From the four hundred fifty applicants, only the top twenty would be accepted, and the entrance exams took place only once a year, during the month of September. That meant that I needed special tutoring and, of course, my Godfather was willing to finance it.

31

How could I not give it a good try? And a good try I did! It was really ironic, because I tried so hard, studied so many hours, that my poor father started to change his approach toward me. All his life he was the type of a guy that would keep telling me, "Study, study my son, so you can become somebody". I remember so many times, we would be walking down the streets of Athens and he would point to a shoeshine guy and say to me, "Do you see him, do you want to be somebody like this poor man?" But nowadays he was so concerned about my health that the same man, in the same voice, would say to me, "Slow down son, you are doing too much, you are killing yourself." But I had to; there was no way to go through this without an excessive amount of studying. I heard rumors that made me wonder if I would ever be able to make it (some said there were many people who tried three and four times to get accepted into that school); what a horrible thought!

At the tutoring school I realized how little I had learned during all those years in high school. Was it because I was not smart enough? Was it because of the lack of good education caused by the war occupation of four years? I did not have an answer to those questions; all I knew was that I had to struggle and struggle I did. Month after month I would find myself submerged in the idea of doing everything I could to get into the University. Giving up all social life and any recreational activities was the hardest thing for me to endure.

The class room in the tutoring school was small, and included fifteen students. The teachers were so dedicated that you felt some special attraction to the whole process. For the first time in my life I realized that I was really learning math, chemistry, and physics. WOW! This is something!

A month before the exams, our teachers started to prepare us for the tests. They had a way to evaluate our progress, or the lack of it.

We all felt that we definitely had made some advancement, so did the teachers, but to what extent? Who would ever know that?

Finally the day came, ready or not, there I was in that huge auditorium, totally lost, surrounded by hundreds of students, all looking for the same chance to do well and get accepted into that school.

After that day, the longest weeks came and were gone until the day arrived when the results were posted at the main Hall. I rushed to the University as fast as I could. I remember looking at that board, my eyes popping out hoping to see my name there but it was NOT. I did not make it. I found out later, by request, that I was forty second. Not good, but not that bad either.

From here on the future looked kind of questionable. But I was not about to give it up. After all, I had all the support of my family. I had to go for it, try one more time, and that I did.

The next twelve months were the longest and trying months of my life. Going back to the tutoring school and hitting the books was first priority. The worst thing that happened to me was that I could not participate as much as I wanted to in the activities regarding our place in Kavouri. Since here it was, that beautiful place, totally destroyed by the Germans, and we had to rebuild it from the ground up. By now the new place was much improved and was a lot more popular. Everybody was out there enjoying it except me. I would only go there for a break for a few days and my heart would shatter every time I had to leave. But I was not about to let this stop me! I remember being home alone, my book of chemistry under my arm, trying to memorize those chemical equations to the extent that the pages of my book were falling apart. My parents by now started to be very concerned. My mother noted that I was losing weight; her idea was that I better give up the studying. But no, I was not going to do that!

I had an idea; I wanted to find out for myself to what extent I was better educated now than when I left high school. I called the principal and I asked if I could take another final examination so that I could improve my final grade in my High School diploma. Sure enough I was able to take the exam and I raised my grade from C+ to A-. That gave me some relief; maybe this time I could get into the University, I thought to myself.

The weeks and months went by a lot faster now, I felt that I was getting there, but I wanted to do more. I went to the University and I asked to get a copy of the text book of freshman college Chemistry, so that I could study it and be better prepared. I was able to get it; I studied it for a long time and it turned out that, because of the extra effort, something very exciting happened during the entrance exams!

Here it is. The day of the examination arrived. The same routine, same place same everything. Except this time I knew a lot of the questions by heart. Only one question I was not sure I had the right answer to. It was about the famous Canizaro reaction, (which was stated in the text book). I walked to the supervising professor's desk and asked him if it was a Carbon or Oxygen I was missing. Well, he refused to answer of course, but he seemed surprised that I knew the name of that scientist, to the extent that a few minutes later he came to my desk and asked me to get up. He looked around me, indicating that I was perhaps trying to cheat, and he left empty handed and somehow embarrassed. That event made me feel really good. I think I have a chance this time, I said to myself.

The exams were completed; I was a lot more optimistic this time than the previous one. A few weeks later the results were posted, and, to my surprise, my name was not there; I failed again, I thought, but did I? I was not about to give it up so easily. I went to see the chemistry professor the one I talked to during the exam. To my surprise he was so pleased to see me. He started "You have no idea, Mr. Mourelatos, how glad I am that you asked to see me. Let me tell you that three days ago I requested a special meeting of the Chemistry department in your behalf. You had the highest grade of entrance examination in the history of this department, but due to the fact your grade in literature was low it brought your total down a bit, to the extent you were the twenty third in class and", he continued, "I had to argue that as a head of the chemistry department I am interested in having chemists in my class not literature students". "But", he stated to me, "all is not lost, because they are in the process of extending the number of accepted to twenty five students". Sure enough a few weeks later I was informed that I was officially accepted into the Chemistry Department of the University of Athens.

Now I could concentrate on my plans for the future. I started going to classes. I walked into that huge auditorium with about a thousand other students, looking around, and trying to understand what I was really getting in to. The teachers here were a lot different, I thought. No time for small talk, down to business! No time for any questions. There was that enormous blackboard used up from one end to the other with all kinds of formulas, equations, symbols and so on and so on. You have got to catch it, I mumbled to myself.

So, between working for the airlines and going to the University, my time was much filled up. My first break came when I was given the opportunity to fly to one of the most beautiful Islands of Greece, the Island of Rhodes. Now that was something! My first flight ever, going to this famous place, checking into a luxury hotel and ready to party hard, and party hard I did! Too bad these things don't last long and don't come our way more often, I thought.

Rhodes was an Island of choice for many people. It was well known not only for its natural beauty but also for its historical marvels. Because of its geographical location, seated between Greece, Turkey and Egypt, over the years it was sought after by many invaders and was conquered by Byzantines, then Turks, then Italians, and finally in 1947, was awarded by treaty to Greece. Of course its natural beauty, those incredible sandy beaches and the multi colored ocean waters were only part of the reasons people considered it the best place to visit. Coming in to Lindos Port you had to pass through the remains of the statue of Colossus of Rhodes, which was devastated by a powerful earthquake many years ago. All and all, from the surrounding villages, the colorful flowers, the fabulous hotels, the nightclubs, the restaurants and the type of people, both local and visitors, you had a feeling you just wanted to be there forever, only if one could! But I had to move on.

It all seemed as though everything was going just as well as it could possibly happen to anybody who tried hard and also had some good luck. But things don't always stay the same. In my case it was a change a bit faster than I had anticipated.

One morning I received an envelope in the mail which changed everything for me. I was drafted into the Greek army and there was no way that it could be avoided.It was not that I resented being in the army; but I was all ready to start something meaningful in my life. On the other hand my belief was that as I was seeing life by now, the military training does wonders for a man, helps him to mature faster, teaches him to be more responsible, learn about discipline and be a stronger person; so all was not bad.

A few months later I said goodbye to my family, who were obviously traumatized, my poor mother showing her true feeling, crying hysterically, and my father trying so hard to avoid showing his grief. But it was something every young Greek had to go through.

So, off I went, to the unknown world of the military. My hair got a crew cut, took showers with dozens of strangers, being yelled at for every movement you make and going to bed (after an exhausting day of training) in a large room with dimmed lights, trying to sleep on a straw-made mattress and with a group of people you have no idea where they came from.

The basic training was not bad. The food was about as good as expected and I was feeling happy about my progress regarding adaptability to the military life. One exciting thing that did happen stays in my mind. It was that on a somewhat rainy day, my sergeant told me that I had visitor at the gate and the captain gave me permission to go there to meet whoever it was. To my greatest surprise there stood my sister, Rena, carrying my accordion on her shoulders, smiling at me with her eyes wet from tears. She had traveled by bus almost three hours dragging that thing, which, by the way was not very light. How could I ever thank her for that? How could anybody do something like that unless they have beautiful feelings and great deal of love; well she obviously did love me, I thought. But, (as I started to reminisce at that moment) the honest truth was that we had such a unique relationship in our family, (not that we never had any arguments, in fact we had our share of that kind of thing,) but love was the paramount emotion among us. We would all go out parting together. A lot of times my sister, my brother and I would go out to dance and have a great time together. Rena was about four years older than me. I was the youngest, and we had developed an honest bond together. Here is an example that will show to what extent we blended together. One evening, right after dinner, we told our parents that the three of us were going for a walk. That was nothing unusual, of course, but it was not the truth that time; we were going out with our sister so she could meet her boyfriend in that particular open field, so they could do whatever clandestine encounter they had in mind, while my brother and I were seated behind a mount of rocks and boulders, and by so doing offering them some privacy. But there was a reason for this slight "transgression". Our father would "NEVER" allow our seventeen year old sister to go out at night, to be with her boyfriend, not in those days, not in our kind of family. Those memories came to me when I saw her standing there holding my accordion. What a sight! It turned out that my sister's gesture opened new horizons for me, because not only I was able to amuse myself, I also entertained other soldiers as well. It turned out that my captain had a love for music and sometimes he would ask me to go to his office and play for him, which of course resulted in some privileges for me.

The weeks and months started to roll by fast now. One day we were asked to fill out a questionnaire regarding family history, educational background and so forth. To my surprise, a few weeks before completing my basic military training, and before I was to go out to a military unit, I was informed that I was eligible to attend a special military academy of officers with the objective to be commissioned to a second lieutenant. This meant that my total military obligation would be up to three years, but also I would be receiving pretty good pay, so of course I accepted it.

The military academy turned out to be very interesting, although at the beginning, I have to admit, it was very frightening. There we were about a hundred soldiers coming out of this boat, in this strange place, and we were received by the senior class of the academy, yelling and screaming at us like we were an ignorant bunch, or criminals or both. This is a place for some people with problems, I thought to myself. What am I doing here?

That environment continued for days and weeks. All you had to do was to look surprised, ask any questions, move the "wrong" way and you would find yourself on the floor doing pushups with your rifle until who knows when. If your bed was made with a slightly "irregular" look the sergeant in charge would come and rip it apart, so you had to do it again and again and maybe even again, depending on his mood! The training was, however, very beneficial to our physical condition. Running, jumping, moving heavy logs, and so forth, was the routine part of the training, besides the war tactics, to the extent that, for the first time in my life I discovered that I had some muscles. "Now you look like a man", I thought to myself.

The total training lasted six months. During that time I came to realize that I had gained and learned a lot. I formed an opinion of myself. I found out it is more rewarding to be responsible for your actions and not to pass problems to someone else, and you must try to find solutions and answers to all the difficulties you are faced with. I found out that leadership pays handsome rewards, and respect for achievement is part of a true and strong man. Also, during those months I made life lasting friendships including my leader and teacher, a lieutenant from the regular army, who at the beginning I thought was so rough, I started to believe, maybe he is "nuts", but I was terribly wrong. He turned out to be a wonderful human being and a very responsible soldier. Graduation time came faster than we realized. We were now officers of the Greek army and ready to go to our post, but where? What part of the country? We were given a short leave to visit our families, which was very beneficial. My family seemed very proud, obviously, and we had some fun together. But the leave was over as fast as it had started. My orders were to report to that particular train station, on such a date, for my next destination. After traveling for three days, I found myself reporting to a camp, located in the very northern part of Greece, to a town named Kavala.

Imagine that, I was now in charge of a platoon, sleeping in a tent, having my own butler, eating at the officer's cafeteria and doing all kinds of military training and promoting new military tactics. During the weekends we would go to town for some entertainment, with some restrictions of course. The best thing was that the salary we were receiving was practically all going to savings, because there was not a place or a need to use it. What an economical way to live, I thought. Few months went by and one day the Major in charge of the camp called me to show me some papers and explained to me that I was transferred to a new unit. What a surprise! He showed me the map of northern Greece and pointed out the particular location. It was so far out that it would be impossible to find it unless you had some knowledge about the area. It was actually on the border of Greece, next to both Turkey and Bulgaria. That area was kind of dangerous, he explained to me, because there was some residual activity from some communist insurgents, coming mostly form Bulgaria, which at that time was under communist government.

So, now I was in charge of true fighters, a bunch of rugged soldiers, very seasoned and knowing how to go after guerrillas. My quarters were under a bunker in an old fortification, which was built many years ago. The only excitement we have had there was when my soldiers were out hunting for food and they brought back a bunch of rabbits and some wild birds. They cooked them, and we had some good meals to last for a while. The closest I came to danger was one morning, when a trap that my soldier had set up for animals, had caught a wild bobcat by one leg and I foolishly tried to go near it. Fortunately, my guy was near me, and he sensed I was in trouble and he yelled at me, "Boss, look out", and before I knew what was happening, he took his rifle and shot it. I could really have gotten hurt.

40

One day, all of a sudden we heard voices coming from down below the hill, all kinds of people asking questions, yelling for information, asking who was in charge here, and how they can come to us. I sent down my sergeant and asked him to try to find out what was going on. Sure enough, in a few minutes, I received a shocking surprise. Here he was, my brother, Rico, climbing up towards me, looking exhausted, haggard, and very hungry, in his Greek uniform. It turned out, since he was about to end his military duty as a private, he was given his last leave, so he decided to use his free time and come all the way up to this Godforsaken place, just to be with me! I just could not believe what was happening. How did he ever found out where we were? I thought to myself, something must have happened back home, was somebody sick? It took him three days to find me. But that was my brother, always standing by my side, always showing me how much he really cared for me. What other brother would ever make this type of sacrifice? It was unbelievable!

That assignment lasted only a few months however. One day I received notice to move back to central Greece to work with groups of civil defense which was more relaxing and more fun, working mostly with civilians and living in very comfortable quarters.

My assignment was basically to travel on foot, from my base to numerous villages, which was practically a whole day affair. It was such a fascinating experience, going through such fantastic natural wonders, crossing rivers, climbing some rugged mountains, and walking through some narrow paths, all alone, without any company, except nature's whispering mystic like sounds, the kind I never heard before in my life. The villagers were always so hospitable. They would gather around me, mostly the notables, starting with the Sheriff, then the Priest, the Mayor, and the man in charge of civil defense. They would start bringing me up to date for any activities in which they had some concerns and needed some, if any, military assistance. By and large everything was routine, their life was so peaceful and they seemed only too happy to see somebody from the civilized world! The remainder of my days with them was mostly social, with good and plentiful food, "first class" quarters, and a lot of gratitude, which made the whole, long trip, tolerable for each and every village I visited.

But like anything else in the military life style, things were constantly changing. So the next thing I heard was a new transfer for me to the most exciting place I could have hoped for. My assignment was to report to the headquarters of the Central Military Command in Athens, i.e. the equivalent of the Pentagon in U.S.A. That was something that neither I, nor anybody in my military circle could believe. I had a suspicion that my father had put some pressure on some of his contacts to bring me closer to home, but of course my good performance as an officer must of have helped some. Imaging myself in that fabulous place was something I could not have possibly conceived, other than in a dream. I had never thought that packing my things would have been such a sweet experience. It all had happened so fast. Before I new it, I was on a military plane flying to Athens. My family was so thrilled to see me knowing that I would be home from now on and after almost two years of absence we would all be together again.

When I reported to my base, which was near the main building, I was offered a huge fancy desk, an assistant, my business telephone and my private telephone, (very unusual for a military person) and of course my private quarters, to be used only when on overnight duty. The rest of the days I was free; yes free, to spend the nights at home! Now that was so unbelievable. When those instructions were given to me, it sounded like music to my ears. On the top of that I would be eligible for the use of a Jeep and my private chauffeur for any official use.

Now, regarding my assignment, it was too complicated, too detailed and too much paper work that I was not cut out for. I was not the sort of person who would enjoy doing that type of work, "This is not for me," I thought. Basically what I was supposed to be doing was to arrange for supplying every high status military officer with every conceivable office needs: from desks, to typewriters, to copying machines, telephones, chairs, mirrors, chandeliers, you name it! All they had to do was call me and ask me for whatever they needed, and I would have to find a source and arrange for ways to supply them with that, only upon signing a receipt of a voucher, a copy of which I gave to my supervising captain and keeping one for my own file. The work was not hard but I felt that I had an enormous amount of monetary responsibility, but I had no other choice but to do my job.

Everything was now so much more enjoyable. I had regular office hours, for lunch I would go to that exclusive officers club and after work I would go home, change to civilian clothes and out I went for fun and partying. Every other week I would have to stay overnight at the base to supervise security; other than that I was free to go home. But being young and foolish I had my share of wild activities. One of them could have caused me a lot of problems. So there I was one night, on duty, and in a prearranged schedule with the civilian chauffeur of the limousine of the Army Chief of Staff, I left my post and went out at the gate where my good friend "George" was waiting for me in that beautiful black limousine. He introduced me to his girlfriend "Katy" (who turned out to be the maid of one of the army generals) and her friend "Olga", and off we went. My suggestion was, of course, to take a drive to Kavouri, and I received no argument from them. Fortunately we came out of this without a hitch. The next day, (as I was lying in bed at home trying to get some sleep), I started to sweat while I was thinking how stupid I was to even dare to do what I had done the night before. I was counting all possible causes which could be held against me if somehow I was caught. To start with, I left my post, then without authorization, I used the General's limousine, and then I was entertaining civilians while on duty, and so on and so on. What a foolish and irresponsible act! "How lucky you were no to get caught", I said to myself.

One special, side assignment, that we were given, from time to time, was patrolling the streets of Athens, looking for any type of misbehavior of any military personnel. I would walk the streets observing and taking notes and at a given time I would meet with a certain General at a certain spot to report any major infractions. It was very interesting, at the beginning he would come out of his Jeep, we would talk for a while and then off he would go, since there was nothing to report, but after not too long, as we would meet at a certain spot, he would only open the door to his Jeep and state, "I don't think anything has changed, has it?" and my answer was, "No Sir". So, off he went. But I remember one particular time, when I encountered a situation that I had to report. Here it was, a young soldier walking downtown, alone, his hat sideways, his shirt totally unbuttoned, slightly intoxicated. I stopped him and asked him a few questions. Since I did not wear a special outfit he had no idea that I was more than a regular Lieutenant and he started to be a wise guy. After I explained to him what my assignment was, he almost fainted, but then he acted like a lamb at the hearing against him, where he faced some minor charges.

Military life now was more routine and much fun for me, I really felt that this assignment was pure luck, I was having regular work at the office, I was meeting important military personalities, I was treated like someone special and on top of that I had a good social life with a few extra "drachmas" to spent, or to save. By now the idea to go to

America was growing more and more in my head, so I started building a savings plan, mostly in gold coins. That was, until the day I received an envelope directly from the Army Chief of Staff advising me that due to my good record of service I was to report to that particular Advanced Military Academy for training on the most advanced and sophisticated weaponry of the times, and after my discharge, (in case of war or any emergency) I would qualify to be promoted automatically to a captain.

That had a double effect on me; for one thing it would change my good fortune of pleasurable life style, and, on the other, even if it was a very flattering event, the timing for transferring to that Academy was short. I figured that it would be impossible for me to have time enough to transfer all those invoices to my successor and remove my name from records to a responsible assignee. The first thing I did was to talk to my supervising captain about it. His response was a typical bureaucratic type, i.e. "Just start looking into it and you'll see what happens," he said. However the days were coming and going and I was short of hundreds of cases in which I could not find the right invoices to transfer them successfully. My next step was to talk to my major, the head of the department. I got the same response all over again. By now I was a few days from reporting to the Academy and I was really concerned. There was a lot of money involved here and if left, I would be held accountable, if I could not find somebody to receive and sign and accept responsibility for all those invoices which were unaccounted for.

"You have to make one of the most important decisions of your life," I thought. And that I did, indeed.

Three days before reporting to the Academy, after a sleepless night, I got up that morning, took a long shower, put on my best uniform and went straight to the office of the Chief of Staff. Since practically everybody knew me there, I did not need a special clearance. The Chief was in an important meeting, so I had to wait almost half an hour. Finally, that huge door opened up, and there he was, that big belly general walking out, surrounded by a dozen military brass, looking at me. I stood in front of him, almost allowing him not much room to go around me, and with the strong military voice I had learned in the past, after a forceful salute, I announced my name and explained to him that I had received his order to be at the Academy in three days, but it was physically impossible for me to do that, because of my position and logistical reasons. After he had spent a few seconds trying to assess what I was talking about, he looked at me straight in the eyes and said to me, "My young man, I want to find out what is this all about," and then he returned to his secretary and stated, "I want you to look into this matter and report to me immediately". After that I left, wondering what I ever accomplished. But it didn't take me long to find out about the ripple effect of my action. A few minutes after I arrived at my office I got an urgent call to go and see my captain. The moment I walked in I knew he had heard about my morning meeting with Chief of Army. He was furious, his eyes popping out, his mouth trembling. As he was trying to talk to me, his face was the color of ripe tomato, he was holding a file of invoices while pointing them to me and saying, "What the H.....are you trying to do, stick those things on me? Are you out of your mind? You will never get away with this." Just as we were about to start an argument his phone rang. I heard him say to the person on the other side of the line. "Yes Major, I am talking to Lieutenant Mourelatos right now; we will be right there." He took a deep breath, opened the door and I followed him upstairs to the Major's office. To my biggest surprise the whole episode started to look like the situation was turning towards my direction. I got the feeling that whatever was discussed between the Chief of Staff and the Major, was in my favor, to the extent that, after the meeting between the Major, my captain and myself was over, the outcome was that the captain would sign all the unaccounted invoices, so that I would be free to go as soon as I was able to produce the list of invoices in question. It was agreed however, that I would be permitted to delay my enrollment in to the Academy for a few days, after a special authorization from the Army Chief of Staff was issued.

Finally, all that mess was resolved; with receipts in my pockets of all the items in question, with all identifications, such as, item description, serial numbers, invoice numbers etc. I was finally ready to go. When my father questioned me about the outcome of that affair and, I in turn explained to him about my encounter with the Chief of Staff, he was speechless, but he came out with a good one: "Son, you have now become a MAN", he stated with a sneaking smile!

Saying goodbye to my family has become routine by now. I was on a train trip to a place called Evria, about two hours away. Nice ride, beautiful scenic areas, lots of sprawling farms of wheat, corn, and lots of olive trees.

As I came out of the train I saw in front of me a huge building that looked more like a College campus than a Military Academy. "What a classy place!" I said to myself.

Since I was about a week late I had to move faster than anybody else, trying to catch up with what was going on. I noted that most of the instructors were Americans working with interpreters. The weaponry was obviously the latest, complicated and very sophisticated. "Do you guys already know a lot about this stuff?" I asked my classmates.

The whole thing was very exciting; you were looking at weapons that had not been tried in any operation before. The class was almost like a science or electronics room, very fascinating, very unusual, a non-military type setup. But, it was a routine life style.

One afternoon the mail soldier came to me and handed me an envelope, the type that looks very important, very official which keeps your mind moving fast in all kind of directions. It took me a few minutes to come to themain part of it, trying to remove one envelope layer to go to the next. "This must be some important document" I mumbled. Finally I was able to get to the core of things. It was from my Major of the Central Operations Office requesting me to produce invoices of such and such items with such and such I.D. "Oh boy! I hope I have a good answer to that, I hope the list of the receipts which my captain had signed includes those items now in question" I said to myself. Sure enough, I rushed to my room, opened my briefcase, looked at the list that I had kept with me and there they were, all seven of them, and they were perfectly identifiable. My suspicions and concerns had paid dividends, and they were worth thousand of dollars. All I had to do now was make a copy and submit it with a letter explaining that my responsibility had ended after said transfer was completed and signed by my captain, and that was the end of it, I never heard anything more on that subject.

The training here was very much unlike the boot camp and the officers academy, very little physical exercise, many hours in classroom, some homework and plenty of time for entertainment. We were given weekends off and we had a chance to go home to visit our family.

After three months, graduation time came. We had a small ceremony, were awarded our graduation degree, given our next assignment, and two weeks leave. Although I was pleased with that honor, I got a big disappointment. My hope was that I would return to the Central Military Command, but that was not the case. Instead I was to report to the boot camp of Heraclion, Krete as a recruiting officer.

After two weeks of rest and relaxation with my family, here I was flying to Crete thinking that perhaps this would be my last transfer. After all, according to regulations, in one year I would have served three years and then I will be eligible for discharge.

Heraclion is one of the most beautiful cities in this historic Island of Crete. It is located on the northern side of the island, right by the Mediterranean waters, loaded with natural beauties, great beaches and very enjoyable climate. The people here are the most laid-back type, very cordial, helpful, and basically very happy.

I was received here with some kind of status. Maybe they have received a copy of my credentials from my attendance in the last military academy and were impressed, I thought. My post was to be an assistant to the captain of a forty-eight men company, who were here for basic training.

It is very hard to describe the impression I got during that particular assignment. Here you are receiving a bunch of young men, who are coming to you from various parts of Greece, from different backgrounds, some of them totally uneducated, hardly being able to read and write, not even being able to count from one to ten. Some of them, (which were the most impressive) were the ones who spent all their young lives up in the rugged Greek mountains as shepherds, trying to keep their goats and lambs from being attacked by wolves. How on earth can you take that type of person and try to build in him some confidence, discipline, coordination and judgment, so that you could trust him to carry out a simple function such as of holding a rifle? Let alone preparing him to go out and fight a possible enemy and also to be able to protect himself from harm and come out alive?

But yes, you see in them the incredible change day in and day out with small steps, a tiny progress today, and more obvious progress next week. First they are able to walk in harmony, and then they are able to understand basic military functions and principles. By now they know what discipline is and why it is necessary for the company as a whole as well as for their benefit and safety. They learned how to stand up straight and show some pride for the way they function, and for all the things they've learned. I never thought that I would receive such an enormous satisfaction from observing such an obvious improvement in those young men. One has to go through this to fully grasp that feeling.

Every day now I saw myself more and more involved in this type of activity to the extent that I started enjoying it so much that I couldn't help thinking, hey, maybe this is my call in life, maybe I could join the regular Army and be a professional soldier. But as fast as those thoughts came to my mind, just as fast they were replaced with my profound interest to go to America and become a success.

You see, now I had some free time to think about America. I started putting all my salary into original financial plan, and I started counting the days, one at a time. By now I was having some serious thoughts about it.

After looking at American books and magazines, I realize the need to learn English; I only had a few English classes when I was at the Central Command. I felt I needed to jump in with both feet on that matter, but it seemed so difficult. I was wondering how my life would be, moving so far away, to a strange world with a different way of life, a different type of culture, with all that wealth, so many cars, so many tall buildings, what New York really looks like at a close distance, how can I manage without my family, how would they take my departure, me traveling so far away? All those thoughts were now sinking in to me. Somehow I had to find some answers.

Six months came and left and we had the satisfaction of completing basic training for the company, along with about a thousand soldiers from the camp. Now that was such an overwhelming thrill! Just looking at those men walking out from their buildings in perfect formation, with obvious confidence in themselves and such strong desire to show how proud they felt with their accomplishments. That made me feel so good and pleased, knowing that in a small or large degree I had contributed in part, to see the improvement in those young men's lives. I was worth every effort I had made in that process.

By now I was entitled to a short leave and with some of my associates decided to visit the City of Hania; we rode a bus out there and spent a few days wandering around those old ruins.

On our way there we stopped at the ancient and historic city of Knossos to visit the famous Palace of King Minos. According to excavations, the area was inhabited since Neolithic times, about 6000 BC. The most fascinating part of the whole complex was the ruins of Labyrinth, in which, the mythological Minotaur, half man half bull, man-eater was imprisoned.

Our visit in Hania was very short and very pleasurable. The people there were typically friendly, farmers, and fishermen. Significantly tall, handsome men were the norm rather the exception.

The new recruits arrived on time as expected and we started our routine training program. I felt that by now I would have no surprises and my job would be just as rewarding this time as it was with the first group of recruits. Finally, after a little over three years, the news came that I was about to be discharged.I must admit that I had mixed emotions about the news. Of course I was expecting it, but somehow, now that it was facing me straight on, I was not too sure how to receive it; the hardest part was to answer questions of my staff as well to some of my troops, who for one reason or another had developed some closeness with me. "Are you going away now, what about me, what I am going to do without you from now on?" they would say to me, while their wet eyes would look at me, as to make me believe that a direct answer was in order. Frankly all I could think was that I was not too sure I had a good answer to those facial expressions. But hey, "I am a soldier; sentimentalism is NOT a requirement in the military life, so move on."

And move on I did. After a small ceremony, five associate Lieutenants and I received our discharge papers and with some degree of emotional shake-up we parted ways. I was now in a plane on my way to Athens, going home to my family, but for how long?

From the moment I got off the plane I felt something unique, something difficult to explain, not even to myself, let alone to talk about to others. My first thoughts were, "So now what? Where do I go from here?"

After all the welcoming celebrations were happily completed the two most important steps were in order. First, to report back to work for the airlines, which by now had some considerable improvements and expansions, and there was not any question about me being rehired with a good pay. The second one was to report my discharge to the University and start going to classes. I must admit it took me a while to adjust to my new lifestyle; it all seemed so unrestricted, so leisurely and non-performing, that I found the need to put myself in a different gear and start doing some serious thinking. But the more I tried to find ways to get some fulfillment in my new life, the more unanswered questions I had in my head; the main thought always being, what about

America? I needed an answer, some sort of indication that somewhere, someone, or something would come about to shift my direction more clearly and indeed it came sooner than I had anticipated.

It was the most unusual day for me. There I was, on my way to the Chemistry class and somehow, that day, I felt the need to skip the first session and go to visit my chemistry Professor. I think his name was Dr. Zervos, the same person who encouraged me to stay in touch with the University, and who had asked me not to lose hope of getting in. It was not too simple though; he was in the Laboratory and I had to wait for almost an hour before seeing him. Remarkably enough, although he was dealing with so many students, he remembered me, not my name, but my face. "Come to my office" he said. There I was trying to think of what to say to him, and where to start? What is it that I am trying to accomplish here? I did not have an answer. I took a deep breath, looked him straight in his eyes and started talking

"Professor, the reason I'm here, "I said", is to ask for your help. I have just being discharged from the army, started my classes and I am really enjoying it. My Godfather is an industrialist and believes I will have a great future as a Chemist in this Country, but for some reason I feel very strongly that I would rather go and study chemistry in America. I have saved enough money while in the army and I have a distant relative in America who would help me to obtain my student visa. So, I want to ask you for your opinion and I trust that it will be very straight forward and very helpful to me."

Well, never in my life have I had such a powerful response to anything I requested. He was sitting behind his desk, just listening and as soon as I finished talking, he got up, went around that big oak desk and stood in front of me, and stated: "My young man, you tell me about having some ideas and some means to go to America to study chemistry, and you are having second thoughts about it? Do you realize that we have hundreds of students in the chemistry department? Even if you were able to finish classes after four years, you would have to wait three more years to finish your Laboratory studies. That would make it seven years before you would be able to work in the chemical industry and even then you would only find a job in a soap, or wine company, "washing test tubes". If that is what you want, fine. Now, my advice to you is if you are serious about America, pack up as fast as you can and get the h.... out of this school".

All I could say was, "Thanks Professor, you helped me more than you can possibly imagine, and I will always treasure you being there the day of the entrance exams, your encouraging words to me to never give up on my struggle to be admitted into this school, and now you are helping me make my next move towards the most important journey of my life". And with that I offered him my hand and with some hidden emotion, he grabbed my hand with both of his hands, and with shaking voice he wished me "GOODBYE AND GOOD LUCK."

That was the indication I was looking for. Obviously, without that kind of a booster it would have been difficult, if not impossible, to make up my mind on what I really wanted to do with my life.

Now that the decision was made, things started to move smoothly; it was like rolling down the hill on a bike. The plan was to make contact with various Colleges and Universities in America and see which one, if any, would accept me, and if I had any choice, where did I want to locate myself?

So, after a number of applications and correspondences, I was finally accepted in St. Mary's College of Moraga, California. I was attracted to it by the size of the school, a small college of about seven hundred students; the very welcoming letter they sent me, stating that they had an international group of students and they were looking forward to increasing its size, and that I would fit in very well with their projected plans. I would be living on campus and would have some personal attention. Also I had some distant relatives in San Francisco as well as in San Jose, just in case of any emergency.

The time to obtain an American Student Visa was here. First the acceptance confirmation from St. Mary's College, then the application to the American Embassy, with affidavits of support from American relatives and then the examination in English. As a requirement, you must know at least five hundred English words to pass the test; I didn't know that many and was concerned I was not going to make it, but somehow I passed.

Everything was going as well as expected and on schedule, but bad luck got in the way. About two weeks before my departure I took my girl friend, (which I had met in Crete and she came to say goodbye) for a ride in my brother's motorcycle to Kavouri. Everything was going well, until half way there, a big truck made a left turn, just as I was passing it, and without any warning whatsoever, and before I knew it, I was on the ground, with bruises on my face and legs, and my girlfriend sitting by the side of the road, totally unharmed, thank God. I was more embarrassed than hurt. I called my brother, and of course, being the kind of brother he is, his main concern was how I was, never mind that his beautiful bike was crashed. "I'll take care of this," was all he said to me. He looked at my girlfriend and asked her if she was okay. He took us to the urgent care clinic, where I was treated, and put on crutches and we were on our way home before I knew it. Now my brother had a plan. When we arrived at home, my parents were down the street, visiting our relatives, so he chose to ask ALL of them to come to our home, pretending to show them something unusual, knowing well enough that my mother would be hysterical seeing me in such bad shape. His plan worked very well and after their original shock, everything somehow turned out fine.

My concern now was how I would be able to do all the necessary preparations, such as visiting the American Embassy, travel agencies etc. But somehow I managed very well. The closer to the date of departure, the more anxious and unsure I became. To make matters worse my Godfather wanted to see me and my father. As I was looking at them, they were asking all kinds of questions. "Do you really want to do this? Do you know how much you will be missed here? Is it not too far away to try something like this?" And so on and so on. I was so impressed with their concerns about me and my plans, that for the first time in my life I knew I was doing something worth noticing and that felt good! Before we parted, my Godfather took me close, hugged me, and said in a very emotional tone: "Look Lalas, let me tell you this; since you really want to do this so badly, go give it a try, but if for some reason you find it difficult, or impossible, I want you to promise me that you will not push too hard and that you will ask to come back, and all of us, me and your family will be happy to have you back." When we left him I was not too sure that session had helped me or made it more difficult for me, but all and all it was okay.

The program of my trip was all taken care of; the Greek airlines gave me a free ticket to Rome, from there I would travel by train to Naples, where I would embark on the Andrea Doria Liner to New York, spend one day there and then fly to San Francisco.

What I had bean dreaming about forever was now become a reality. I was not totally sure that I was prepared to face all the obstacles, but one thing was very clear in my mind: I just had to try it and I was ready to move on!

# CHAPTER 4 – Flying to America

Without any more complications or delays the big day came. Here we were, family and friends at the Athens airport. All I remember was, that my mother and father were in a very frightening emotional way, trying literally to stop me from boarding the plane, crying so hard I felt that I was really hurting them, but that was not my intent, not at all, I just wanted them to be proud of me, and that gave me strength I needed to climb the stairs to the plane.

I remember looking out the window as we were taking off, and with tears in my eyes I whispered to myself: "I hope you know what you are doing, I wonder when you will see this land again, if ever... what about them" (thinking about my family). Finally the clouds surrounded the plane and there was no more visible sight of any land, it was all gone, lost in the mystery of my attempt to go to a new and different world, to fulfill the dream of my life. I just started thinking right there and then, "You are not running away from anything, you are trying to get somewhere." That made me feel good inside, I grabbed a magazine and started reading just to get away from the sentimental mood I was in, and I kept reading until the stewardess leaned over to me and said: "You look like if you could use a drink". She was right on the mark at that time and for sure the drink felt good going down!

Crossing over the Ionian Sea was unusually smooth and we arrived in Rome right on schedule. I was able to spend only one night in Rome, and I didn't have much chance to visit all the sights that city was famous for; but for the few areas that I saw I found them very much as impressive as they had been described in books and other sources.

I really enjoyed St. Peters Cathedral, the Coliseum and some other smaller places, not having much time to see all I wanted to.

The next day, on my way to Naples by train, I had a relaxing and enjoyable  trip, going by some beautiful sites, ancient buildings, farms, and  some vineyards, which seemed to go on and  on for hours. "We are going through wine country", someone said to me in broken English.

I don't remember the name of the Hotel I checked into, but it was a typical seaport hotel, nothing fancy, but very convenient and walking distance to the ship. I had a good Italian dinner and a great night's sleep.

Next morning when I woke up I looked out the window and there she was, that enormous-size ship, Andrea Doria, waiting there, looking like a huge multi layer building and I thought to myself, "Can this thing really float?"

It was an unusually beautiful winter day, and, if I remember correctly, it was about the end of January. The sun was bright, the air crisp and smelled like a typical port, salty, fume filled type ambience. I took my small suit case and started walking toward the ship. The port was very crowded with people and cars all over the place and you could see an enormous amount of ships, large and small, mooring on the side of the port surrounded by thousands, if not millions of noisy seagulls. Going to the gate I was met with a huge crowd of passengers, mostly Italians, typically excited and noisy, but basically happy and ready for a long trip to America. After all the necessary formalities, passport checking, ticketing, etc, I found my way to my cabin and walked in, kind of surprised that it was so small, a double-decked type, something I had not expected. "I have a roommate", I mumbled to myself.

After familiarizing myself with the cabin I decided to go look around, sort of investigating and touring the ship. What an unbelievable experience that was. First of all, I found out that this trip was her second one across the Atlantic, since her maiden voyage had taken place on January 4th, 1953. I looked around in awe; I have never seen anything like this in my entire life, all this luxury, so much gold. The curved stairway to the ballroom was covered with what seemed to be a rich looking red carpet, a huge beautiful chandelier which hung right in the middle of the room, and so many pictures of famous people decorating every wall. It looked like a true palatial place and more. (As I am reflecting on all this now, after over fifty years, I can't believe that this incredible, luxurious, and considered almost unsinkable ship went down on March 1954, after she was struck by a Norwegian ice-breaker outside of Boston).

We sailed about mid afternoon; everything was just as well as expected. The Mediterranean Sea was unusually calm. But after we crossed the Rock of Gibraltar and entered the Atlantic Ocean it was a totally different story. Before I knew it I started feeling strange, my stomach was upside down. I got out of my cabin and wandered around, everything movable was tightened with ropes: chairs, tables, even that huge grand piano. I went back to my cabin and the next thing I remember was that, (after I had called for help), I was given some medication, and then rushed to the ship's infirmary. It turned out that I got so dehydrated the doctor had to give me shots to keep me going. A few days later the weather got better, and so did I!

I was able to get up and move around. I still remember what that nice Italian doctor told me when I was doing a bit better: "You see, my young man, most of sea sickness is in the head; you just have to make up your mind that you are okay. Besides, do you know how much fun you missed out there, missing such a good food, seeing wonderful shows, and dancing with those pretty girls?"

In two more days we would be arriving into New York and I was all excited about seeing that big city.

Coming into the Hudson River and looking to our left, the sight of the Statue of Liberty with its awesome size overwhelmed me. "Just the way I dreamed about it" I said to myself. As we approached Ellis Island I glanced out there and saw all those cars, by the hundreds, moving along in harmony, and also so many tall skyscrapers. What a sight! "Finally you are here" I mumbled.

Spending a few hours going through Immigration and other formalities seemed very easy and simple. I took a taxi to my hotel looking around in disbelief. Truly, my neck was hurting by looking up at the sky trying to get a good perspective of all those enormously tall buildings. What a city! I sure wished I could spent more time here but my limited finances only allowed me one night in New York and the next morning I was on my way to LaGuardia Airport for my flight to San Francisco.

The flight to San Francisco was very long. In those days the plane had to make two or three stops on the way. So after nine hours of flying, with one stop in Dallas, and another one in New Mexico, we arrived in San Francisco around nine o'clock at night. My mother's sister Tina, and her husband Owen, picked me up at the airport, and we were on our way to their home in San Jose, about a half hour drive from the airport. As we were riding on the freeway, what impressed me the most were the lights, those millions of lights all around us, like I had never seen before! This is so different in comparison to

Greece, I thought. I spent a couple of days with my relatives in their nice and comfortable home. What impressed me the most were the supermarkets; I would go there and look around and my eyes could not believe all those products and supplies and stuff that they were selling there. My favorite thing was the ice cream, the variety of it, and the relatively low price, it seemed like I could not have enough of it!

Then came the biggest moment of my entire life! It was Sunday; if I'm correct the date was February 9, 1953. I was twenty seven years old, driven to Moraga, California, about thirty miles east of San Francisco. The ride was just perfect, beautiful scenery, unbelievable freeways and most amazing, those thousands of beautiful cars. As we were going over the incredible Bay Bridge, we saw on our left side the breathtaking sight of one of the wonders of the world: the Golden Gate Bridge. Traveling further east we saw some picturesque hills, and after going through a much elaborated tunnel, we arrived at the small town of Moraga. We were going toward the hills when all of a sudden, hidden behind them, we saw the silhouette of this very charming Chapel surrounded by a number of big buildings. All around us we could see colorful hills, covered with bright green grass, where hundreds of cows were roaming peacefully. "This is your new home" I said to myself with some sort of a knot in my throat.

This is Saint Mary's College where I would try to find out what it means to go for the impossible. At this point I started feeling some sort of desperation, but it didn't last long.

As we walked to the main building some of the students sensed that we were kind of lost and offered to assist us. When we explained to them that I was there to start school, they got very excited and asked how they could accommodate me. So there came Brother Ralph, the man in charge of dormitories supervision, introducing himself in a kind and humble manner, explaining to us, that this being Sunday, all the administration staff were out and all I had to do was follow him to my room to settle in for the night and next day I could start the process of enrollment, classes assignment and so forth. It seemed so simple. Also, to my surprise, he stated that dinner would be served at the main restaurant at 6:00 PM and I was invited to join the students who were in campus that day, and of course I accepted the invitation. I said goodbye to my aunt and uncle, and then Brother Ralph asked one of the students to help me with the suitcase. I felt it was very nice of them and I followed them to the third floor of one of the dormitories and to my room. I thanked the students for their help and they all disappeared.

Now I was alone in this strange room unpacking my suitcase, checking the mattress, peeking inside the closet, trying to locate the restroom and looking out the window to see what kind of view I had. I was pleased to see a well manicured garden, loaded with beautiful flowers, healthy looking trees, well kept buildings, the charming old Chapel, and in general, a beautiful campus. All of this spoke very highly of the quality of people living and working here, as well as the high level of the administrative efficiency to run the College.

I decided to lie down and stretch my legs. I didn't really know how long, when I heard a knock on the door. I opened it and there were two smiling students extending their hands and introducing themselves and asking me if I wanted to eat with them at the campus restaurant, and from what I was able to understand, they wanted me to joint them as their guest to a movie. Of course I accepted. That felt good; somehow I needed that kind of welcoming attitude more than anything else.

A few minutes later, after washing my face, I followed them to a place called "Sala". When that huge oak door opened there was an enormous room with very high ceilings, sparkling parquet floors, and large expensive paintings on the walls. It looked so royal; "Is this the restaurant?" I asked with disbelief in my face. "Yes", they both said. "Here we have breakfast, lunch and dinner every day, seven days a week". What a relief, I didn't have to think about where I would find a place to eat! That set up was new to me; it was buffet style. They walked me to the food stand, handed me a tray and then I followed them and started selecting what seemed good to eat, "This is a fine set up", I said to myself. We sat together at the table and they started asking questions about myself; they seemed impressed that I came from Greece and that I had chosen the field of chemistry. As soon as we were through eating, one of the students, I remember his name was Michael McKierman, asked me to follow him to his car where we joined two other students, and off we went, to the movie theater, about half an hour's ride. I had no idea what kind of movie we were going to see. We got to the theater and as soon as the film started to roll, I started laughing. It turned out that it was one of those scary movies, about alien beasts attacking New York. "Hey, I saw this movie a few months ago back in Greece" I said, "But that is okay."

My first night in the dormitory came and left without a hitch. After so much excitement I slept like a log. I got up about 7:30 AM, took a long shower, got dressed and went straight to the Sala for breakfast. After a short chat with some of the students I picked my tray (the way I learned the night before), I found an empty table, sat down and started eating. Other students sat at my table, asking all kinds of questions with a keen interest about me and my background. I enjoyed all this very much; it made me feel like I was now on stage! After breakfast I went to my room, brushed my teeth, grabbed the necessary documents and went straight to the registration office. The truth of the matter is that I was not too sure I was prepared for the events that would follow in my attempt to register.

After I introduced myself to Mrs. Crawford at the registration office and presented her my papers, which were found in order, the subject of tuition fees came up. She explained to me that the net cost for the semester was seven hundred dollars. All I could do at that point was to look her straight in her eyes and with a trembling voice I tried to explain to her that, due to the cost of the trip, all I had left was thirty nine dollars. The rest would have to wait until my parents sent me some money. Understandably, she looked at me with an expression of total amazement. She stood there for a minute, speechless, and all she was able to say was, "But Mr. Mourelatos, in your letter of acceptance you stated that you would be able to finance your studies with help from your parents. Is this untrue now?" I had to think fast for a good answer but all I could say was, "I am afraid that it turns out to be impossible for them to do". She took one moment to collect her thoughts and said to me, "Please wait here one minute" and then she disappeared.

She was only gone ten minutes, but it sure seemed to me like an eternity. I was in that fabulous office, seated in a very comfortable leather chair, my hands sweating like I just came out of a Turkish bath, looking at the door she disappeared from, hoping she would return soon with some encouraging news for me.

The moment I saw her coming out from that door I felt a big surge in my heart. With a big smile and positive voice she told me that she had just talked with the President of the school and he suggested that they would enroll me now and work out the payment plan as we go along. I almost felt like getting up and kissing her, but, on a second thought, all I came up with was a very expressive THANK YOU, and a rather forceful handshake. Then, after all the paper work was completed, I said to myself: "Wow, finally you did it! Now you are enrolled in the Chemistry Department of Saint Mary's College".

This was a Liberal Arts School, the curriculum besides Chemistry, Physics, and Math, included a number of other courses. However, since it was run by the Christian Brothers, Religion was a mandatory full semester course. As elective classes I took English, Classics and Psychology.

My first class was at 9 AM, the subject: English, which seemed to be what I needed the most. Needless to say, I was lost most of the time, but I managed to get through it. The next one was the true test of my attempt to study what I was there for; it was the chemistry class. We were about fifteen students; the professor, Dr. Jennings, walked in and immediately started to dictate to the class the topic of some kind of organic chemical reaction, explaining the terms to us, problems and so forth. I started to shake; I could not understand anything he was saying; he kept describing verbally the subject matter but I was totally lost. Then he went to the blackboard and wrote chemical symbols, such as H20. CHOH + CL + CO2 etc, etc. Suddenly my eyes opened up, "Well, now I understand what this is all about, this is my territory" I said to myself. Nevertheless the total process seemed like a huge mountain facing me and I was not too sure I had a way to climb it.

The chemistry lab work was a disaster. I had to run a simple titration test to determine the acidity and/or the alkalinity of a simple solution, but I had to read the instructions first and that needed some doing.

This was my new life, in a nut shell. So many challenges and question marks, here and there. How I was going to manage all this? A few weeks went by with the same type of trial and error and things didn't look any brighter.

One morning I woke up feeling very weak and dizzy, I told Brother Ralph, and he immediately took me to the nurse. After she examined me she took me to the infirmary and asked the doctor to come and see me. He run a lot of tests and his diagnosis was; "exhaustion". He ordered me to stay in the infirmary for a few days, prescribed some medication and promised to check with me soon.

I was half asleep when I heard someone coming in. I opened my eyes and there was an older man in black robe with white collar, wearing very thick glasses, standing next to me with a grin in his face and with a very gentle voice said: "I am Brother Beed Edward; I hear you are not feeling well. What seems to be the problem?" I raised my head a bit and I started to explain my situation; that I came here to study, but I didn't know much English, I didn't have any money, my parents could not help me, but I definitely didn't want to give up all my dreams and return to Greece. He looked at me with a very kind expression, and he grabbed my hand and with a slight smile he said: "My young man, what are we going to do with you now? We have to figure something out." Then like lightning had struck the room he raised his voice and asked me, "Would you like to work?" and continued, "I am in charge of the placement bureau, and my job is to find work for the students who are in need for work, and there is plenty to do around here". As if something under me pushed me up, I jumped and without hesitation I replied: "Oh brother Beed that might be the answer to all my problems". He touched my head gently and said. "Get some rest now, gain some strength and we will take care of things for you", and he disappeared before I had a chance to thank him.

A couple of days later I was up and around, went back to classes and things seemed slightly better. Brother Beed left a note asking me to see him. He said there was a job for me the coming Saturday if I wanted it. "Of course, anything will be fine" I said. He told me that a lady would come and pick me up at 9 o'clock to do some yard work at her home.

There I was waiting in front of my dormitory. A woman arrived right on time in her Cadillac convertible, asking for me. I jumped into her car and off we went to her house, about a twenty minute drive. She asked about me a little bit, and then we arrived at her beautiful house. She took me to the back yard, showed me what I had to do, gave me a shovel and a pick, and then she showed me the place to go and "change" my clothes. She was surprised when I explained to her that my flannel slacks and my handmade leather shoes were all I had to wear.

There I was working in this fabulous garden removing weeds and dead leaves, slip splashing in the mud, my flannel slacks full of mud, my leather shoes all scratched up. But who really cared, I was working and making ten dollars a day. Around noon she offered me a nice lunch, and at 4 o'clock she took me back to school.

Now my whole perspective had changed. I had some ways in which to start planning my future. I can do both, study and work at the same time. After all this is America!

A few days later I received a letter from my parents with a 100 dollar check. I wrote back, and explained to them that everything was fine here, and besides going to school I also had a job and I didn't think it was necessary for them to send me any more money, and that I could manage very well. This gave me such relief; after all, 100 dollars was the equivalent of three months rent for them.

Life in campus was now very much a routine. The students treated me really well. They seemed to wonder how I was able to manage; as far as they were concerned, I was doing something totally amazing. At no time did they make me feel unwelcome or treat me like a stranger, even knowing that I was a foreigner and that unlike most of them, I didn't have any financial means and, indeed, I was struggling. On the contrary, they seemed so interested in me and wanted to get to know me better and offered to help me.

One night, while in my room, it was midnight and I was studying chemistry for next day's test. I heard voices from a bunch of students who were calling my name from the parking lot, and before I knew it, they were knocking on my door, rushed in, all excited to see me with my chemistry book on my desk and the English dictionary next to it. They said "Harry, what are you doing up so late?" I explained to them about the exam and that I wanted to be prepared. Wow, they got so excited and started, "You G.......... Greek, you must be out of your mind, here we are, we speak English and we can never understand all that stuff and you think you can do it?" "But of course I can do it", I said, "I have been dreaming about this for many years". They turned around and left, laughing all the way out the door while saying, "Good for you, and good luck tomorrow."

The days and weeks started to roll by now, I began to feel more confident, my English started to improve rather rapidly and I was seeing the many possibilities I had in front of me to make it here. Financially, things looked pretty good. Very often I went to the business office to deposit more and more money to pay my debt, first the 100 dollars I had received from home, and then the few dollars that I had accumulated from work.

By now I was participating in many school extracurricular activities, such as going to the basketball games, playing soccer, playing tennis, joining the other students at dances, which they called them "mixers", in order to meet girls, (at that time the school had only male students,) and many other activities. In short, I could now say I am ONE OF THEM.

I must admit that I was receiving special attention from the good Christian Brothers. My math teacher, Brother Domenic, observed during classes that I had a difficult time understanding a few things; he would ask me to go to his room after class. He would spend considerable time tutoring me until I understood a lot more than I could ever do on my own.

There were many occasions, especially at night, when I would find myself alone, walking around the campus, looking at the bright stars and the beautiful California moonlight, and thinking about my family, remembering the good things we did together, and I would start wondering if this is what I really wanted. How good it would be if I could just be home for a little while to share with them everything that was happening to me. But those thoughts would vanish just as quickly as they appeared.

It was now the last week of May. The school was about to close for the summer and most of the students would return home until September. I was able to accumulate quite a few credits with a pretty good grade average and my account was short by only a few hundred dollars. I had to find work during the summer and make enough money to pay back what I owed and to have enough for the next year. Fortunately, my aunt was able to accommodate me in San Jose and while I was staying there I found all kinds of jobs, from picking apricots, to working as an usher in a movie theater. But, the best one was as a box stacker, in a fruit canary factory, making a bundle of money, and as a bonus, I was developing huge muscles!

Now it was the middle of September and I was back at school. The first order of business was to go to the registration office and pay off the balance I owed them from the previous year, so that we could start all over again for the 1953-1954 school year. Needless to say the business office lady was speechless when I handed her all that money!

This time, Brother Beed had something better for me. He got me a steady job in the cafeteria of the faculty. In addition to the weekend's yard work; financially I was pretty much okay. On top of that, the lady in the business office advised me about the possibility of receiving a student's grant, based on my special situation, all I had to do was to apply for it, which I did, and sure enough, a few months later I received a two hundred dollars grant. Not bad!

The weeks and months started passing much faster. I felt good about my progress. Also, by some good luck, a very good friend of mine, Parry, from back home, decided to transfer from in upstate University in New York to St. Mary's College and that made life easier for me; we both studied Chemistry and helped each other a lot.

Here is something for the books. It was now the Christmas Season. One day Brother Beed called me and asked if I wanted to make some extra money. Before I knew what he had in mind I said "But of course". Well, with a kind of sneaking smile he revealed the whole plan. "The Chamber of Commerce of the town of Lafayette," he said, "wants one of our students to work as a Santa Claus. All you have to do is go to the local Fire Department and they will supply you with a Santa's Uniform, a pillow and stuff, and you will be going around different stores doing the routine Ho-Ho-Ho, and then park yourself in a designated store, so that the kids will come to visit you and you sort of make them believe you are real Santa." The prize was 200 dollars for the whole two weeks! I jumped from my seat; how I could be so lucky? I will never forget how much fun I had while I was making so much money. The thing I remember the most was that the kids, while seated on my lap, and I was talking to them, would turn to their parents and say, "Mom" or "Dad", I don't understand what Santa is trying to tell me". The parent's answer would be, "Well you see dear, Santa came all the way from the North Pole and over there they speak a different language." That was something else! I guess I must have done pretty well because the whole thing was repeated in 1954, 1955, and 1956.

Everything is totally under control now, school is going good. I am learning a lot, months going by and I was feeling great. But one particular afternoon, sometime around March, 1954, Brother Ralph asked me to go with him to my aunt's house. He stated that he didn't know what exactly was going on. We drove all the way to San Jose, about a one hour drive and I kept asking him if he had any idea what might be the reason she wanted me there, but he had no answers. Finally we arrived and the moment I saw my aunt I knew something was really wrong. She grabbed both my arms, she squeezed me close to her, crying hysterically, and told me in a loud voice: "My dear Harry, your uncle just killed himself". I was speechless and confused; all I could think was the times I had seen him totally drunk and out of control. He had been in the military and I gathered that he had very hard times and he became an alcoholic. The explanation I got that night from some friends was that he came home from work early that morning, and after he drank a whole bottle of wine he wrote a loving note to my aunt and then he went to the garage, took his loaded rifle, put the barrel in his mouth and blow his head off. I remember the next day, as I was out there in the garage cleaning up things; I found parts of his brains, laying there, what a horrible sight!

Brother Ralph returned to school and I stayed in San Jose a couple of days trying to be as helpful as I could for her.

I went back to school and I realized more and more that the whole concept of the Catholic religion started to appeal to me. Many times, after classes, a bunch of students on the way to their dormitories would stop for a moment in front of the Statue of Virgin Mary and would pray, "Hail Mary Mother of God,.... and so on and so on", and almost automatically, I would stop with them, stand in silence for a few minutes and then all of us would move on our separate ways. That whole scenario happened so many times that it became routine for me. Of course being Greek Orthodox, my beliefs were very similar to theirs. As a matter of fact, the question was raised by some students about the possibility of me converting to Catholicism, but Brother Beed, being such a wise old man, came out with a good answer: "You can convert a Jew, a Mormon, a Muslim, or even an Atheist, but you can never convert a Greek to Catholicism". But ever so slowly I would feel really good going to Mass in that incredibly beautiful, Old Chapel. Sometimes I even prayed, which has always been difficult for me to do.

We were in the middle of April and mid term exams were in full swing. One Friday, after diner I sat down to study and get ready for Monday's test, when a bunch of students walked in, all excited, yelling at me, "Come on you dumb Greek, let's go to the dance at Providence Nursing College; they have a mixer tonight. Who knows, you might find your future wife there". What the heck, "I will go with you," I said. "Just give me ten minutes and I will meet you downstairs", and off we went.

This was not my fist experience with mixers, but for some reason, that night I felt different, maybe because of all those Nuns hanging around, supervising the nurses to be, made me feel like, "you better behave now, things are strict here".

After we familiarized ourselves with the surroundings, we students started to part our ways and soon enough I found someone to dance with. That didn't go too well. I tried somebody else, that didn't do it either. So I stopped for a while and started looking around. "There is someone I would like very much to get to know," I said to myself, I looked again and there she was a redhead, tall, full body, statuesque, my kind of woman. I approached her and started talking with her. After a small chit-chat, I loaded myself with courage and asked her if she would like to dance with me, "Yes, I would", she replied, as she was leaning toward me. I felt like I was about to lose my balance, which is unusual for me. After all, dancing is my only natural talent. After a couple of dances, we found two empty chairs, sat down and started to have an interesting conversation. I found out that her name was Mary Lou Moore; but when I told her my name, she found it a little confusing. The name Harry was easy, but she had difficult time with my last name. "Mourelatos?" she asked, with a surprising look, "What kind of name is that?" "It is Greek", I said with a quick response, hoping this will impress her. Fortunately she thought it was an interesting name and took it very well. As I was sitting next to her and spent some time looking and studding her, all kinds of thoughts went through my mind. I had been in America almost two years now and for the first time I was close to a woman reflecting the personification of my dreams, the type of American woman who I had seen so many times in the movies, the likes of Doris Day, Betty Grable and so forth, and I was now so close to one like them!!! I started thinking "You better put yourself together before you make a fool of yourself".

After more informal talk, we got up and dance again. I felt the urge to hold her close to me. When I found the nerve to do it, to my surprise she didn't object to it at all! A few minutes later we were getting very close, as if we had known each other for a long time. At that point I was brave enough to give her a kiss, and to my surprise, she didn't object. I felt like I had wings and was ready to fly. Everybody was having a great time, and by now most of the boys and girls started to leave. Mary Lou and I walked to the front patio. I held her close to me, very close in fact. I leaned closer and kissed her goodbye, and then she disappeared to her dormitory. I turned around looking for my ride back to school and in few minutes we were on our way back.

I sat in that car and, although the other guys were talking out loud about the good time they have had, I was in total silence all the way back to school, feeling like I was in a dream and hoping nothing, or no one would wake me up.

Now, I have to state here that whatever took place that very night, caused my whole life to change literally from top to bottom. It was like so many different doors were opening for me. What if I really fall for her? What if this is the woman who is the right one for me? Is it possible that I can be so lucky to be with her forever? How can I afford her? I am just a student, a foreign student to be exact!

I started seeing Mary Lou more and more. We went to parties together, to basketball games, etc. and each time we did, it seemed that we were getting along very well.

One day someone offered me the opportunity to purchase a car, an old telephone company car, a two passenger Ford coupe. If I remember correctly, the price was sixty five dollars. All it needed was a paint job, from a typical company car of, black and olive green color, to something like red, which I thought I could do it myself, and so I bought it. Imagine me now! I have a beautiful American girl friend, a car; I'm doing well in school! What else do I need?

We are about at the end of May and school is ready to close for the summer. I am now getting ready to go back to San Jose and work at my old job stacking boxes, while living at my aunt's home making good money and saving a lot. Mary Lou would catch the bus from time to time to spend some weekends with us. Our relationship was getting more serious and we felt very good about each other, besides having a great time together. However, I noted that when it came to the subject of romance, she seemed rather inexperienced, innocent, almost naive, so I had to be very careful and patient. But "So be it", I said to myself, many times.

The summer of 1954 was over now and around the middle of September I was back to school. Having earned good money, I was able to pay off my account again, (to the surprise of the business office lady) and I was back to the whole routine of things.

All was well until some time in November when I received some startling news. Mary Lou's mother, who was stationed in a Naval office in Hawaii, had convinced Mary Lou that upon her graduation, due in two weeks, to go and stay with her for a while.

I received the news with mixed emotions. For one thing I was happy that she would have a chance to go and visit that incredible place, do fun things, meet different people. I tried to encourage her to meet other guys so she could be surer about her feelings toward us. On the other hand, I felt the pain of distance and how much I was going to miss her. But if that was what she wanted to do, it was okay with me.

Now what? Mary Lou left and here I was, trying hard to keep myself busy, doing all the necessary things I had to do, doing my home work, studying and working. The thing that matter the most was our correspondence. I was so happy to receive her letters, even when she was telling me about her social life. She even mentioned that she had met this nice guy and they were going here and there, and in parenthesis she stated: "Isn't this what you wanted me to do?" I wasn't too sure how to take it, but nevertheless she was honest with me. But in a strange way she would say that she was not happy being around her mother, which I found very odd, but I never questioned it. I, for one, had no idea what to make of it; it seemed so unusual for me to hear that, since I had such a good relationship with my parents, but at any rate that was the way it was.

The Christmas Season came and left in a hurry. I was very lonely but I managed.

Sometime in February, I received a letter from Mary Lou informing me that her mother would return to the States and she decided to stay there and work at the local hospital. Now I was crushed. This was bad news for me; I didn't know what to make of that, "Something is wrong here" I said to myself, but again I didn't question it. I was very confused. I felt the need for answers and some guidance. For the first time in my life I would go to Church kneel down and pray, asking God for help. I decided to go and talk to Father Dominic, a very smart and kind priest. I walked to his room and there he was, wearing his all white Dominican robe, looking at me with a curious face. He asked me to sit down and I started pouring out my soul to him. The best thing that came out of this meeting was his suggestion that I should try to stay in touch with him and talk about my emotions during the coming months, which, he believed would be a trial period for Mary Lou and me. That's what I really needed, and it indeed helped me enormously.

All I could do now was to stay in touch via airmail and also call her a couple of times, explaining to her that I was in love with her and I could only wait for her to make up her mind and come back to me.

The good news arrived a lot faster than I expected. Around the middle of April, she wrote to inform me that she would be coming back to the States to work at the Providence Hospital in Oakland and we would be back together soon. I was now in heaven!

After her return, it didn't take too long for Mary Lou to show me she really loved me, to the extent that it was her who actually asked: "When do you think we can get married?" I was so surprised when I heard that, I didn't know what to think. I didn't know if I was happy, confused, scared or the combination of all those feelings, but I started to do some serious thinking. My first step was to talk with Father Dominic. I can still remember to this day his reaction. "She has asked you a very important and sensitive question; don't you let her CRAWL", he told me with a very serious tone in his voice. That was the encouragement I needed, and I made up my mind right there and then.

We talked some more about it and we set the date for September 15th, 1955. The plan was very simple; would get married in Oakland, and rent a small apartment there. I would commute to school, she would be working as a nurse and I would be doing my part time work as usual.

After the semester ended I went back to San Jose and returned to my old job. This time however, since my aunt had decided to go back to Greece, I needed to find a place to rent. My friend Parry and I found a place together and all worked out fine.

When I went back to my old job, I told the news to my boss that I was getting married in September and I asked him to help me with overtime work, and of course he did. I was working so hard and so many hours that I didn't realize that by end of August I had put in the bank over 1200 dollars.

I will never forget the reaction of the woman at the business office at school when I walked in to register for my junior year and I handed her a check for 1000 dollars. "This is for the next two semesters" I said. She just stood there, in awe.

Now the wedding preparations started to take place and one of my obligations was to meet with Mary Lou's priest who had some instructions for me. One of them was that I had to promise our children would be baptized and raised in the Catholic Church, and of course I had no objection whatsoever to that. The other was that Mary Lou, being a true Catholic, the only birth control allowed was the rhythm, nothing else. I had no objection to that either.

A few weeks before our wedding, something strange happened and I was very confused about it. Mary Lou had to be admitted to the hospital for a few days. "Just to have some corrective work done", was all that her doctor told me. I never understood the meaning of this, but frankly I didn't even care. I was in LOVE.

The wedding was nice; it took place in a beautiful chapel by Lake Merritt in Oakland. Most of the guests were from Mary Lou's side; I had a few distant relatives and some friends. The only important person missing there was her father, since her parents had been divorced many years. Her mother Pauline was there of course, but not only was she unhappy, she looked pale, as if she had come out of bed with some sort of illness. Mary Lou told me later that her mother was up all night vomiting. That seemed kind of odd to me, but I did not ask why, and there was nothing more said about it.

The reception was at her aunt's house and everything went very well. My best man was Roger Hill, a good friend from school who was always close to me. After the wedding we were to drive to Carmel for a few days and then, all the way to Los Angeles. However, for some strange reason, when we were ready to leave for our honeymoon, Roger took me by my arm and in a peculiar way he said "Harry, please be careful and gentle with her!" I heard him, but I had no idea why he said it and why at this particular time. I just thought he wanted to be a good friend. But was that all to it?

Before our drive to Carmel, we stopped for some last minute shopping Mary Lou had to do. I will never forget that moment. I parked the car on the side of the department store, waiting for her as I was leaning against the fender. I watched Mary Lou walking down the street. Every man that she passed would turn around and look back at her.... Her red hair flowing down her shoulders; she was wearing a long blue dress and walking as if floating... She was so beautiful!

Our ride to Carmel and then to Los Angeles was just as simple as it could be; the only exciting thing happened when we were on our way to the hotel. The muffler of that old telephone company Ford car of mine fell off, right there on Hollywood Blvd., so we had to stop and fix it. Fortunately, it occurred during working hours.

Our honeymoon was just okay. No fire works, kind of simple. "She is so inexperienced, I have to be patient with her", I said to myself. "It will get better".

We were back from our honeymoon. Mary Lou went back to work and I returned to school. Everything seemed all right, except her fear for intimacy and pregnancy. I, for one, could not understand her concerns. After all we were married, and personally, I wanted children, many of them, ten would be fine; after all this is America and in my mind, it would be easy to raise kids here, and I could provide for them. But something was not right.

One day Mary Lou had some concern about her health; she went to her doctor and found out that she was pregnant. She was not too sure that it was good news. According to her doctor, she could not have a normal delivery, and would need to have a cesarean section.

Again I received the news with a stoic attitude, "If that is the way it's got to be, it will be okay" I thought to myself and I was happy. I was going to be a DAD!!!

It turned out the pregnancy made her feel good; she seemed happy with the idea of motherhood, and things were rolling along pretty well. One day I received some interesting and somehow frightening news from Greece. My brother, Rico, got married a Greek-American girl and was planning to come to the United States. I had such a confusing feeling in my heart. For one, I was happy that he was married, hoping that it will be a good thing for him; but, on the other hand I felt a tremendous fear for him and his future. I started wondering what chance of success he could have. How could he possibly manage to make a good living here? To begin with he had never shown any interest in America. He never learned English and my understanding was that his wife, Mary, was expecting a child. We had no means to help them. At that time we were living in a small studio, and our finances were down to the minimum, how could we possibly help them?

Time went by, and before we knew it they arrived at Oakland Airport, Mary carrying her child, six months pregnant, and all they brought was a small trunk and about ninety dollars. Where could we accommodate them? Fortunately, Mary Lou's mother, who was living in a two bedroom apartment in San Francisco, offered to let them stay there for a while until they found a place to live. Our distant cousin, Peter, was able to help my brother find a job and soon enough they found a place of their own. They were on their way to a new, and as it turned out, a very successful life.

From our side, things were moving right along. Our baby was on its way and according to the medics it was going to be a healthy baby. So, it is August 31st, and my first child was born, John Mourelatos, who was named after my father. I will never forget how beautiful Mary Lou looked after the delivery; she had an angelic look on her face, walking down the hallway at the hospital, wearing a long white silk gown, just as if she was trying to say, "I have done the impossible". That was the kind of expression on her face.

I was up in heaven when I first saw John wrapped up in a white blanket and all I could say was "Is this a baby?" and the nurse said, "Yes it is, and it is yours".

I still remember driving John home (to our newly rented apartment). Every time we went over railroad tracks or potholes I had to make a full stop, to the obvious amazement of his mother, like "What are you doing that for. He is not going to break". But to me that fear was definitely there.

What followed was a good feeling for both of us. She was such a good mother; being a nurse had its advantages. I was the one with all kinds of anxieties and concerns. I had to learn to be not only a student, but also a father. Many times she had to go to work at night and there I was trying to study and also trying to feed John and then rock him to sleep. Those were really good times.

My graduation time came faster than I thought. Fortunately I had the opportunity to work, as a gardener, for a wonderful man, Mr. Evans. He was a Vice President for a Manufacturing Company, a large corporation, and of course he had many contacts in the chemical industry. Before my graduation he had said to me that the moment I got my degree I must tell him, and in turn he would try to find me a good job. And he did just that. He got for me a job as a research chemist for the division of Chevron Chemical Co. of California. That was an unbelievable opportunity for me to get started in. My job was to run chemical reactions in order to develop resin products, called polyesters, which were based on a derivative of petroleum. But right after I started working there, being surrounded by all kinds of guys with Ph D's, I realized I needed to do more schooling; otherwise I could not compete there. It was all over my head. I started thinking about going to Stanford University. My Greek friend Parry was already there and had encouraged me to apply, because they had a good size international community and needed more foreign students.

Our second son, Steve, arrived a few months later. We were having a good family life and everything seemed to be fine. A year later Eric was born and about that time it felt like I wasn't going anywhere in my job, I needed more education. I did apply to Stanford University and I was very lucky to be accepted, although my grades were not the best.

I was struggling however to make it. There I was, going to a tough school, and, at the same time, I needed to work part time to make some money. Mary Lou was working part time and things were getting tight. My Professor was a very understanding man, so he arranged for me to work in the laboratory for a German Post Doctorate student, running some routine chemical reactions, marking my time and getting paid accordingly. Fortunately my own lab studies were next door to his, and that made it very convenient.

But no matter what, it turned out that it was impossible for me to continue my studies under those conditions. I was failing on my grades, the exams were more and more difficult for me because I was not well prepared and I started to have second thoughts about being there. Finally, one day my Professor took me aside and explained to me that he realized my position and advised me to consider dropping out. "After all", he said, "you have been going to this fine Graduate school for a year. Unless you want to teach, you should not have any problem working in any chemical Industry and make good money." That was all I wanted to hear. The last thing I wanted to do was to teach.

After some searching, I found a job working for a large paint and resins company. I started making good money, in fact more money than my chemistry professor at St. Mary's College. That did it. After a few months we bought a beautiful home in a good community, near Palo Alto, and I was commuting to work, about forty five minutes distance.

Now we had everything we needed. Mary Lou didn't have to work anymore; we had three beautiful healthy boys, a gorgeous home, two cars, a dog, and a good environment. But something was missing. I had a difficult time trying to figure out what it was. Her mother seemed to be some sort of a problem, something I could not understand. I would come home from work and all I had to do was look at her and I would have to ask "Your mother called and talked to you today didn't she?" And her answer of course was, "Yes." But it always seemed that something was going on that I could not figure out. One of the subjects was having more children. I was told from her doctor that, physically, Mary Lou should not have any more children, because if she got pregnant again she would be torn apart, and I accepted it and promised to do what I had to do to comply with that. It was suggested by her priest that I have to request special permission from the church to have an operation, called a vasectomy. I had not any hesitation whatsoever doing that and I hoped this would solve the problem. But did it?

For only a short time things got a bid better but somehow it did not last long. I started realizing that her breath would smell alcohol, but I had not seen her drinking anything. Sometimes I would look in the garage for tools or something and would discover a glass half empty with booze of some kind. I didn't know what to make of this. Although I had never seen Mary Lou intoxicated I realized she just had to have a drink in order to relax. But she always seemed in some sort of restless mood. I tried to talk to her about it but it seemed that I would agitate her more than help her. Finally it became clear that even with my operation clearing the way for any fear of pregnancy it had not eliminated her lack of a romantic mood. For whatever reason I couldn't know and wouldn't understand, I had a feeling there was a reason somehow, somewhere.

This situation continued for a year or so, and I started feeling like the reverse case of the movie. "The Barefoot Contessa", where this aristocrat met a beautiful lady and falls in love with her, and decides to marry her, but he never discloses to her that during the war he was injured from an explosion and his manhood was destroyed and he could not function as a man. He could not make love to her. During their wedding all the relatives seemed very nervous, obviously knowing well the risk he was taking. It turned out that his newlywed wife succumbed to the temptation and had an affair with the grounds keeper. The rest was history.

I was despaired now; I had to find answers, so I felt that I had no choice but to seek information from her family. I called for a meeting with her mother, her aunt and uncle. The meeting went well, but I did not receive anything of importance, except to talk to her priest for advice.

Now I had to do what was the best for my family. I started thinking about some radical change. I said to myself that, here I am working for this company for four years; I come and go every day, park my car in the same spot, doing the same thing, working in the same lab. This is not what I left my beautiful country and family for. I make good money, my beautiful kids are well taken care off, but my wife is not happy, maybe a change will be good for all of us.

My answer came sooner than I had expected. One day a very smart sales person, Peter, from Boston, Massachusetts, from one of our chemicals supplier at work asked me to go to lunch with him. After we finished our lunch he asked me if I was happy with my work there or would I consider a change. He explained to me further that the chemical product, which his company was supplying to us, was enjoying very good business from us, and he had found out that I was somehow responsible, because I had formulated a coating, a product that was used in many large plants, including Boeing Aircraft Co. I told him that it was my understanding that this was true. Furthermore I explained to him that I had started thinking I had reach a point with the company that I would consider a dead end; therefore I would start looking for other ventures. He stated that he would talk with his people in Boston and see what they could do.

Two weeks later I received a call from Boston and it was from Peter, telling me that he would be in San Francisco the following week and would like to have dinner with me at his hotel. I met with him and he proposed that his company will like to fly me to Boston for an interview, which I accepted. I flew to Boston and after that meeting I was offered a job as a technical service supervisor, doubling my salary, with many benefits, a lot of traveling around the country and all that good stuff.

I flew back home with a good feeling and I asked Mary Lou what she would think about something like that? Her answer totally surprised me. "Anything, just to be far away from my mother will be good enough for me" she said, her eyes sparkling as if she had seen a bright light.

The wheels were now in motion, first to resign from work, then to sell the house and arrange for a home in Boston. Taking them one at a time had its interesting points. My resignation had some intriguing twists. First of all, my boss, the technical director, was putting allot of pressure on me to reconsider, which I found very interesting, because I had asked many times for advancement and raises but I was only being given a "serious consideration." But now their doors looked ready to open for me. On top of that the general manager came all the way from Los Angeles, and among other things, he asked to go out to lunch with me for the purpose of pressing me to change my mind. "What a novel case?" I said to myself. All this time I was just one simple case; now that I am leaving I have become a BIG case. But this is the way the business world functions; they work differently under pressure, which was not for me.

Our house was sold with some profit; we found good buyers for the cars and all the furniture and we were ready to move to Boston.

Fortunately my brother was well established. He started building an estate in San Francisco, learned English, and worked as a designer for an architectural firm and was raising three beautiful children.

On our way to Boston, as we were waiting at the airport to board the plane, with all of Mary Lou's relatives there, as well as my brother with his family, and in a very emotional state, he turned to me and said, "I came here all the way from Greece, just to be close to you, and now you are leaving me to go three thousand miles away, why? I felt a bit sad hearing that, but there was a reason for my going; a better future for my family and that was very important to me. But I could not say anything; I hugged him hard and all I was able to think about was how he had managed to have such a beautiful family, with a good and hard working wife, Mary, and very bright and energetic children,

Mina, John, and Aleco and that he was able to be well established in such a short time. I really felt proud and very secure about him and his future in America. So all I could tell him was: "I am going to miss you, and I wish you happiness with your beautiful family". I held him close to me and with tears in my eyes I said goodbye to all of them, and disappeared. - As I reflect now, this being the year 2006 that some forty six years ago, how was I to know, that by now, he and his very hard working family were able to built a Real Estate Empire, which, in my humble opinion is now worth many millions of dollars! That is, for sure, a great accomplishment and it can only happen in America!

# CHAPTER 5 – Looking for a Better World

The flight to Boston was long but without a hitch. At Logan airport we were, surprisingly received by the Vice President of the company, Dr. Perry and his wife. That seemed like a good start. From there, they drove us to our new quarters, an old Bostonian type, two story house with a big yard, very comfortable looking, "but" with no air conditioner; what a bummer!

After a day of settling down, I reported to work and it became obvious to me that I would be doing a lot of traveling all over the country promoting the company's products from a technical point of view.

The company building was a red brick type, three story, old factory building, which was renovated, located in Cambridge, walking distance to M.I.T. and also walking distance to that magnificent Charles River. From the very beginning it became clear to me that Massachusetts people and from Boston in particular, were, by and large, very smart, educated, and a cultural kind of people. The city of Boston showed many characteristics much similar to those of San Francisco and in many ways it seemed like being back home.

The house which the company was renting in our behalf was large enough and comfortable but not where we would like to stay any longer that we had to. So we started looking for a home, preferably a new one, and we found one under construction in the city of Walpole, about a thirty minute drive to work.

Our new life had now done a full swing. Here we are in this beautiful, brand new, two story home, new furniture, new station wagon, and a smaller one for me, an Opel. The school was walking distance for the kids and the whole neighborhood seemed ideal for family-style life. The church was nearby, shopping was a five minutes drive, and a small lake was within walking distance, which made the kids very excited. Being in Massachusetts, a lake has two advantages; one, it is good for fishing during summer time and two, it is good for ice skating during winter time. Who could ask for anything more?

I started to realize more and more that my attention toward the kids was becoming very strong. I felt the need to devote more time and energy to them. Every place we took our kids to we had such a wonderful reception! The comments of friends and associates was so rewarding and thrilling, regarding the appearance, behavior and intelligence of our children.

As the days rolled by, the situation at work was becoming more and more exciting and challenging. My orientation program was very short and the assignments started to come one after the other.

It was only after a couple of weeks that I received my first project, which was to fly to New York for a presentation at a large paint company in Brooklyn. I had no idea what to expect, what to prepare for and what to bring with me. All I knew was that our sales Rep, Jim, would pick me up at LaGuardia airport, and drive me to the customer's plant, where I would make my presentation, go to lunch with the technical director and then fly back to Boston the same day. That sounded very simple to anybody with experience, but not to me. I had never done this before in my life!

To my surprise it turned out pretty good; as a matter of fact, it was much better than I hoped it would be, but also because of what my boss, Dr. Perry, had thought it would turn out to be. What actually happened was that, our Rep called Dr. Perry and explained to him that the technical director of that paint company had told Jim that he would very much like to offer Harry a position in their company. Now how is that for a good start!

My second assignment was a week later and that was a two-day trip to Montreal, Canada. By now I started feeling that this was something which not only I could do and do it well, but I would like doing it. Of course, that was just the beginning of what was part of my job.

By now the summer was almost over. The kids were registered at school and everything seemed much better than our life back in California. We met nice neighbors and became very good friends, and the kids also made some good friends. I tried to encourage John to get in to baseball but I had limited success, he was not ever into sports. Steve, on the other hand, was into everything, so much energy so much excitement, his whole life style was going, doing and more. Eric was too young for much activity, except that he showed some interest in music. After a while I decided to get a piano for myself, and as soon as he heard the music coming from the piano, Eric got very interested in it. So I decided to hire a piano teacher. She and I agreed that he had a definite talent, and his long fingers were what one really needed to succeed in playing piano. Unfortunately, his interest was short lived. When the Beetles became a big hit and guitars became the thing, he lost interest in piano. To Eric, fishing in that small lake was the most impressive thing; even to this day after almost forty six years, he reminisces about those happy days of our fishing there.

One significant difference of the housing in most of Massachusetts communities, especially in the suburbs, was that there were no fences between homes, and it was much more conducive to develop close friendships among neighbors, in comparison to California. For instance, during the summer, it was very common for the people next door, or across the street, to come out in their yard and before you knew it, everybody got together for a chat or a short visit. No invitations were necessary. The same thing applied during the horrible months of winter. Everybody went out of their way to help their neighbors in any way they could, using all the means available to them.

It was now the middle of October, and I was driving to Logan Airport on my way to Los Angeles, for the National Chemical Convention. All of a sudden there were some white snow flakes dropping on my windshield and in few minutes heavy snow started to fall. I could not believe my eyes! I thought that it was too early in the season for that. By the time I arrived at the airport, the roads, the buildings and the trees were covered with snow. "What a novel experience," I thought. I found a parking spot as close to the terminal as possible, having in mind, that I might not be able to find my car when I return from Los Angeles.

Arriving in Los Angeles gave me a strange feeling though. Here I was in this fabulous city, the sky was blue and clear, and the temperature was about eighty degrees. Everybody was dressed in comfortable shorts, or light clothing, and here I was in a heavy winter suit, sweating like a horse after a race. I started to wonder if Boston was, after all, a good place for us to be living.

The convention was full of excitement, lots of displays, many interesting products, and some very new developments, more than one could possibly imagine. All and all, it was a novelty for me, educationally as well as entertaining.

I received exciting news from the kids when I called home a couple of times. "We are having so much fun here in the snow, you can't believe it Dad. Everything is covered with white around us!" They would say with such excitement in their voices. Hearing that made me homesick.

After a week of having such a wonderful experience in L.A. I flew back to Boston. It was Sunday night and the snow was coming down pretty heavily. As I was leaving the terminal trying to find my car I realized how smart it was of me to park the car so close to the main entrance; otherwise I would not have been able to find it; it was totally covered with snow.

It was not until the following weekend that climatic conditions gave us some great opportunities for real fun and joy. About two bocks away from home there was a kind of declining land area next to an abandoned farm which was an ideal place for snow games, such as tobogganing, sliding, and so on. After we had a chance to go and purchase toboggans and sleds, the kids and I walked to that spot and joined a whole bunch of others to ride down the hill, having the time of our lives. Here I was, now thirty six years old, going through some of the most enjoyable times of my life. Just looking at my kids, having an opportunity to do the things I had dreamt about all my life, to be able to see and do, made me feel warm inside. I was looking at them playing in the snow, in such a perfect location, such a serene and beautiful environment, trees loaded with snow, birds flying over our heads trying desperately to find some food, cool air blowing around us, the colorful and warm clothing everyone was wearing, made me think. "Just the way I was pictured it all those years when I was growing up, going to the movies, reading American magazines, etc. Now here I was, with my children, going through it in real life!" It is almost impossible to describe the enormous satisfaction I was feeling, just to be there, experiencing those moments of real joy. It made a huge impact on me and deep in my soul I thought, "This is for me; this is what I was made for and this will never change as long as I am able to be with them and function this way."

There were, however, some interesting differences in the State of Massachusetts vs. California, regarding educational standards. We would have to send John back one year, in order for him to be able to catch up with the local scholastic requirements. That was unexpected, but it seemed reasonable enough, although it did not speak well for the Californians. But it was the best thing for John. On the other hand, the situation with Steve was a totally different story. After a couple of months of schooling, we were called to the school and were told by Steve's teacher that he was not only a good student, but he was a gifted child with a high I.Q. This did not surprise us, since he had such an outgoing personality; he was always in a state of action, always looking for things to do, curious, and restless. I have to state here that this did not go too well with his mother; she would have preferred, it seemed like, that he would be more subdued and less active. She always made a point to make it difficult for him, when he was trying to express himself and be himself. I had a different point of view on this and we had some serious arguments about that many times.

It was now more than a year since we moved to Boston. It became clear to me by now that Mary Lou's situation, mentally and physically, was not improving. I did realize that one of her stronger wishes was to find and meet her father, whom she had not seen since she was about twelve years old. I encouraged her very strongly to find a way to do that. We both contacted various organizations, such as Veterans Administration, Department of Defense, and the Navy, and so on. Luckily, after a few months of effort, it became clear that he was somewhere in California, alive and well. So, in no time, we made contact with him, and before long, he was able to come and visit us.

When I first met Herbert, her father, I was impressed with his good looks and mannerism and his good physical condition. Our son, John, looked a lot like Mary Lou's father. Herbert spent a few days with us and he seemed a down to earth person, and even likable. It was such a relief to see Mary Lou happy for a change, and one time, as we were at a basketball game, I saw Herbert and her talking and laughing, having a really good time; that seemed so heart-warming.

# CHAPTER 6 – My wife's tragic news

My hope was that Herbert's visit would produce positive results, that it would help Mary Lou to recover, and it would have some permanent and positive effects. But it lasted only a short time. Many arguments ensued and things were getting more and more difficult at home.

Now I found myself in a very confusing position. After some serious consideration I decided to meet with our local priest for guidance. It did not take me long, after a few minutes of discussing our situation with him, to discover that I was not about to receive any specific benefit from that meeting. The only direct response I did receive from him was, "Is it that serious between you and your wife?" And then after a small chat we had together I thanked him for his time and disappeared.

It was a very dramatic point that developed a few days after my visit with priest. When I came home, that particular day, I realized that Mary Lou was extremely upset. Nothing was said until the kids were in bed. It turned out that her mother had called, and after Mary Lou told her that she had found her father and he had come to visit us, the whole thing developed into a horrible situation. Mary Lou was so upset, almost hysterical to the point that she really got me concerned. It was like a nightmare, and what did actually develop was the turning point of our life together.

After she had a chance to put herself together for a few minutes she started to spill her guts out to me. THAT WAS A HORRIBLE STORY!

It all had to do with the fact that her father, who had been in the Navy for many years, was an alcoholic, and somehow lost his mental capacity. As it turned out, he molested her, causing her a severe medical problem, and she was only eleven years old. The worst of all, it was her mother's reaction to that terrible tragedy that caused Mary Lou to truly hate her. "The happiest day of my life will be when I BURY my mother," she said angrily, and repeated it many times since then.

The months ahead were the most trying and truly stressful times in my entire life. "Where do you go from here?" I started asking myself. One must be strong to face many difficult times in life. I had the hardest time adjusting to the idea that anybody could possibly do such a thing to someone that they loved so much. I had a very difficult time understanding what was going on, and what exactly had caused Mary Lou to feel so hostile toward her mother? What did her mother do during that ordeal? Did she blame Mary Lou for what happened to her? I had some suspicion that her mother did that, but I was never told that, and had never asked, hopping that some day it would come up on the surface, but it never did. Except one day, after pressing Mary Lou very hard for an explanation as to her difficulties with her mother, she finally revealed the real problem. With tears in her eyes, and in an angry tone she said. "What do you think I felt when, being there on stilts, with everyone watching me, my legs wide open, while somebody was pouring permanganate on me?" What a horrible thing to happen to a young girl! I had to assume that Mary Lou was infected with some kind of venereal disease and they were trying to treat her with whatever medication they had handy. By doing that they must have destroyed much of her private organs, and then I assumed (looking back at the time when we were about to get married), that this must have been the reason her doctor did "corrective work", or plastic surgery to her, few weeks prior to our wedding! I started thinking now, how could anybody understand the trauma that one young girl had suffered during that ordeal? But I was never told anything more than that by anyone, and I did not know why it was such a big secret. If I had the nerve to tell my parents, what my wife's parents did to her they would probably think that I had not used good judgment when I involved myself with the kind of people who have had no connection, no similarities to our standards, and that those people must have been really sick. I felt that it was best for all concerned to keep all of this to myself.

As much as I wanted to avoid being angry with Mary Lou's parents I found myself trying to understand her feelings, her painful background and the misery she had endured all those years. I started looking at her and the way she was deteriorating and all I could think was, how could she possibly cope with all that pain in her soul and the every day suffering, and then I ended up feeling pity for her. My whole world started to turn upside down. Like a motion picture, I found myself thinking back to the days I dreamt of coming to America, the Country that is, and always will be, the place to find happiness and wonderful things that life here can offer you. Where is all that now? What did I miss here? How have things gone so far out in the wrong field for me?

Those horrible thoughts and questions stopped the moment I said to myself, "Wait a moment; I have the most precious gifts given to me that anybody could have asked for, my three beautiful sons, the joy of my life, their smiles, their tender expressions, their confidence and obvious trust in me and the pleasure of their presence." That did wonders for my personal strength and my determination to find ways to go on with what was presented to me for my new life. That perspective gave me the booster I needed to keep on going and find solutions to the problems ahead.

The severe winter came faster than we anticipated. Those "nor'easters" as they call them here, created a worrisome weather condition in the Boston area. However, the good news came that the small lake, walking distance from our home, had been frozen and tested by now, and was safe for ice skating. Imagine that! We went to the store and purchased ice skating shoes for the four of us and we rushed to the lake as soon as we had an opportunity to do that. What a thrill! I had never thought I would be able to get on those things, let alone being able to skate on them. But after I saw my kids, within a few minutes skating around me, making fun of me, (being so clumsy and slow, falling down every two or three steps), I decided to make an extra effort and start showing them that I could skate, maybe not as well as them, but skate, nevertheless. That was what I needed the most, this time of my life. The excitement, the thrill of being with them, and having so much fun! I was so impressed with John moving about on his skates as if he had done this all his life. Seeing my kids and a bunch of all others, having the time of their lives, was such a rewarding feeling, that all of a sudden my trust and confidence in the American way of life rushed to my rescue; it just felt so good.

I feel that is now imperative for me to put down in this writing my activities regarding my association with the chemical industry. Thinking back, about the way I was seeing my way of life then, it was clear that what I was planning to be and do here in America, had turned a corner and I found out soon enough that, to be, "just a chemist, working in a laboratory day in and day out", was not as challenging and as exciting as I had originally thought. That was not me. But, maybe because of my marital problems, or because of my personality and/or my needs, I had to have more of an exciting personal life, (besides the wonderful thrill I was experiencing from my sons' relationship with me). It became very clear to me, that in order to survive, be of sound mind, and be a good person, in spite all the obstacles I was facing, I had to have some job satisfaction. It turned out that what attracted me the most was the idea of being out in the field, making presentations, helping the marketing forces, traveling to various parts of the Country, and I found out that, not only did I enjoy it, but I was good at it. However, I discovered soon enough that these kind of positions, not only in the chemical industry, but in any other industry, are not very stable or secure, simply because, by definition, they are secondary type, or FRILLS related, as they call them, and therefore they depend on the market trends and are subject to frequent turnovers. Nevertheless, I decided from that point on, that I would take my chances and proceed with that approach, because that would give me all the necessary basis to be happy and continue working with VARIOUS chemical companies, if indeed that was the case.

So, now based on those premises, I had taken the position to look ahead for more and more activities of field work and attempted to fine-tune it and even try to perfect it.

"You have to get ready for a big presentation in Chicago" my boss told me one day. This was going to be very important. It was the largest account of the company and I had better be well prepared for it. It turned out that the president of our company, as well as the vice president of the company, who we were about to make the presentation to, were going to attend. Our sales Rep reserved a hall large enough to accommodate about twenty people, for the presentation, as well for the dinner following later on.

We arrived at O'Hare airport around noon that day, giving me plenty of time to set up my props and everything I needed. As the time got closer and closer I was getting nervous, I had no idea had I was about to be faced with. Never before had I made a formal presentation to a high level personnel and started feeling the pressure. The closer to the scheduled time I came to, the more uncertain I became. About fifteen minutes before I had to begin the presentation, I rushed to the nearest bar and asked the bartender for a double Manhattan on the rocks. Being that I am not the drinking type of a gay, I knew I was taking a big chance, but my choices were limited, either that, or I would not be able to function as well as I needed to, and probably would make a fool of myself. So "lets try the easy way" I said to myself.

Now, there I was, in front of a bunch of high class executives, presenting my props, color panels and displays, explaining to them all the benefits of our product, versus the competition, and they seemed, to my amazement, impressed and very receptive. As a matter of fact, I thought the best way to make a good impression was to use some humor. That's why, after the introduction and some details on the topic of the presentation, I came up with this statement to them "By the way, if for some reason you don't understand some points of my presentation, please don't feel bad, there is nothing wrong with your ears, it's just "THAT" Greek accent of mine, that interferes with what I am trying to explain". Well, there was such a roaring laughter from all, and from that point on, everybody was at ease, especially me. I continued with what I had already prepared for them, with colorful schematics and graphs and competitive features, which showed vividly the advantages of our product. They seemed to want to know more, and they had a lot of questions, which I was able to answer to their satisfaction, and which, I believe, is the key to an effective presentation. After that, we had a good dinner, lots of laughs, and a happy ending.

"You son of a gun, you pulled a good one yesterday", our vice-president of marketing told me, all gleaming, as I walked into his office, after he had asked to see me first thing next morning. That was so good to hear!

# CHAPTER 7 - My New Family Visits Greece

The closer we came to the summer time, the more I started thinking about our vacation. I had a very good feeling about the company and also about my performance so far. I began thinking perhaps they would not mind if I asked for an extended vacation so we could go and visit my family in Greece. After all, I had not seen them for over eleven years. Fortunately, my boss, Dr. Perry, was very understanding and when I asked for three weeks of vacation he seemed almost thrilled that I had such a plan and he did agree to it. "Harry, I think it is wonderful that you will be able to go and see your family and be with them after all these years", he stated with a bright smile and a hand shake as I was leaving his office.

The preparations for our trip to Greece were now in full force. Since we had to plan for three weeks vacation, it seemed as a good idea to visit other countries besides Greece. So, first we stopped in London where we spent a couple of days. That was such an exciting time! We came out of the airport, and on our bus ride to the hotel, John started yelling: "Look Dad, we are traveling on the wrong side of the road! What is going on?" And of course I had to calm him down and explain that the British people drove on the left side of the road instead of the right, as we do in America. That impressed him a lot. We stayed at a nice hotel, walking distance to the famous Piccadilly Circle. What a fascinating city! British people seemed very well dressed, fast moving and very polite. I was surprised to hear one man, as he was passing us, mumbling, "Here come the YANKEES!"

Among other adventures, we went to visit the Big Ben, the Underground Stations, and of course the change of the guards at Buckingham Palace. What an impressive tour! The weather was on our side, very unusual for London which is famous for having the most rainy days than any other major city in the world. Our visit there was very pleasurable and educational. The kids were fascinated with the fact that, although the people in England spoke English they had a very hard time understanding them because of that strong British accent. But, after all, "that is the beauty of traveling and visiting different countries", was the best explanation I could have given them.

Our next stop was Paris. Here we were able to spend only one night but we had a chance to visit the Arc de Triumph, the Louvre Museum and the Eiffel Tower, which was a new twist for our kids. "What are they saying here? What kind of language is that?" was their first reaction. What a city! I was so impressed with Paris that I wished we could have spent more time and see more of it. You could feel the culture, sense the presence of artistic excellence, and the rich architecture and musical advances that make this beautiful city famous for. I was not too sure, however, that the kids were old enough or interested enough to grasp what was presented to them here in Paris. Maybe some day we will be able to return I thought.

The next day we flew to Rome where we had the chance to visit some of the most important sights of that magnificent city. Among the excursions we toured the Vatican, the Coliseum and St. Peter's Cathedral. Well, there we were in that fabulous Church and John decided to do what I would consider an incredible act. As we walked in and we were by the stands with those lit candles, hundred of them;

John felt that perhaps there were too many of them, and some needed to be eliminated, so he started, with such concentration, to blow them out one at the time. I must admit that I did not know what my predominant reaction was, curiosity or anger. I grabbed him by his arm, took him out through that huge door, down those large stairs, and really scolded him to tears. "What a guy" I thought, but that was that.

Although I had written to my family that we were on our way to Athens, that particular day I wanted to make sure that all was fine and that they knew the actual time we would be arriving, so I tried to phone my parents, but I could not connect with them. Then I tried to call my sister Rena and happily she answered the phone. Still, to this day, after almost forty five years, I feel that excitement, my heart started to pump faster, hearing her voice, like soft music, the voice I had not heard for over eleven years, saying to me, "So you are coming, you will be here tomorrow! I must be dreaming; how are you, how is your family?" And I could sense that her eyes were wet from tears, her voice trembling, and hardly being able to continue our conversation.... All I could think was, how close I was to be with her and the rest of them, and that gave me the strength to say a few more words before I was out of control, "We will be with you soon",... I said and hung up.

Arriving at the Athens airport was like coming from out of space back to my old world. All I can remember, as I came down the stairs from the airplane and reached the ground, is that my knees seemed to be giving up on me. I knelt down and put my wet lips on the ground, thanking God for the opportunity to be back with my family, in my country, the place which had given me so much, and had made me what I was and had built in me a purpose in life. It taught me to be strong and responsible and also gave me the capacity to love my people with all my heart, all the ones who are close to me, no matter the distance which could separate us. Just as if I had woken up from a dream, I looked up and there they were, all my family, the "Mourelatos Clan", waiting for us, rushing toward us, laughing, crying, yelling, hugging, all at once. I remember my father taking charge of all the arrangements regarding passports, customs, and other official details, making the whole transaction much easier for all concerned. I could tell that Mary Lou and the kids were overwhelmed with not only the large crowd which was there to welcome us, but all the emotional commotion which was developing around them. Somebody did grab John, another grabbed Steve, and still another grabbed Eric. Mary Lou was surrounded by a bunch of people, who were trying to explain to her that she was so welcome in the family, and all she could do, not knowing any Greek, was to give them a warm hug and a big smile. It was obvious that all this welcoming experience was new to my wife and children, but a routine for me. Somehow that seemed very puzzling to them.

We spent the first night at my parent's apartment, a small two bedroom unit, in the old town of Athens, on the third floor, and walking distance to everything. Fortunately it was summer time, the weather was so beautiful, and we had no problem being well accommodated.

Next day, arriving in Kavouri in the afternoon gave me an enormously warm feeling. I just stood there in front of the house, (which had been recently expanded into a roomy, all-stone house), among those beautiful pine trees. Looking over the blue water, with the golden trace of the bright sun laying on it, I couldn't help but think: Where have I been all these years? Am I really here? Is this really happening? Maybe I am dreaming…. Before I was to go any further with my thoughts "Dad, Dad, what place is this? Wow, how long are we going to stay here? Let's go to the beach". To hear this from my kids was all I needed to bring me down to Earth and start planning our staying here. So much to do, so much to see, was all I could think of. The amount of attention we were getting from my family was something difficult to describe. Mary Lou and the kids seemed so pleased with the way they were treated by all of them. They just could not get used to it. My mother was trying to explain to Mary Lou in the best she could, that she was so happy with my new family and wanted to do anything possible to make them feel comfortable and at home. My father, on the other hand, was doing all the planning for all the fun activities, mostly relating to the beach, boating etc. But most of all, he took total control of purchasing all the supplies needed, the way he always did, so that we would have plenty to eat. My mother, being such a good cook, made sure we did have great meals and great service; she just wanted to spoil all of us.

The advantage of the summer weather made it so easy to accommodate all of us. Mary Lou and I were given the main bedroom and the kids would sleep in that enormous front patio, on folding cots. Practically everything, like dinning, visiting, playing games, etc., was done outdoors. Such an easy and relaxing type of life that in essence, was uncommon in America.

Next morning, after a good night's rest and a good breakfast we rushed to the beach. No one can really imagine the sensation I felt being back at that beach, the white sand, the warm sparkling blue and clear water, caressing those colorful and various shaped pebbles, which almost seemed to recognize me. Once being there by myself, I must have forgotten than my wife and children were there with me and I just kept daydreaming, ignoring them, not wanting to be distracted from my beautiful thoughts and the good memories that had come back to me seeing the familiar scenery, but... "Hey Dad, Dad let's go to the water; this is unbelievable," was all I needed to hear from my kids, which would bring me back to the real reason I was there, to show them how good it was for me, and what my life was like in my youth. The truth of the matter is, than even today, after so many years, Eric still remembered when they were in that small boat, and John and Steve were vigorously rocking it right and left, so hard that all Eric wanted to do was get out of it. I took him off and put him on the shallow waters for a moment, but still that wasn't good enough. He grabbed me around my neck and said, "Please Dad, please Dad, take me on shore." So, without wasting any more time, I took Eric on my shoulders and carried him to the beach where he felt somewhat more comfortable. But later on he got used to the whole adventure and started having the time of his life.

After a couple of days in Kavouri we decided to visit some of the historic sights of Athens, namely the Acropolis, the Parthenon, the change of the guards, the museum and few other places which was mostly beneficial to Mary Lou and of small interest to the kids. But we felt, after all, they were here, and might as well take advantage of the time and see some of the magnificent sights which made this country so famous.

Back in Kavouri the activities of fun and games resumed and one of the most amusing things was that Steve decided to become an entertainer; he just felt the urge to perform. One time, right after dinner, with a bit of coaxing from me, he got up on a chair in front of about fifteen people and started to recite a poem. After he finished he bowed with a huge smile. He received a large round of applause from everybody present. That became a big subject of discussion for days to come, because he had made a good impression on all of them. "He must go and try to become an actor," my relatives kept telling me with such an exciting tone of voice, but I had already figured that out! I knew Steve well!

The longer we stayed there the more I realized that since the kids didn't need to go back to school for another two months, it would be a good idea for them to stay here another month or so and I would go back to work in a few days. I packed, and was getting ready to return to Boston, leaving behind me my TOTAL world, and this time a larger part of me. This is the irony of life. How can I explain? How can anybody really be able to grasp my feelings now?

Two days before my flight back to Boston, and with the help of my brother-in-law Mike, who happened to be the general manager of IBM in Greece, and who had many connections, I was able to meet with the general manager of EXXON in Greece. Since he was originally from Boston I thought he could try to find me a position in the Greek Chemical Industry. It was a very productive meeting, but it turned out, everything considered, that, "Harry you will be better off in the chemical industry in the United States than in Greece," I was told in not uncertain terms. That did it, and that door was closed; it was a good try though.

This time my departure from Greece was different. I said goodbye to my people in Kavouri and not at the airport. Doing it that way made it a lot easier for me. I felt that a part of me was staying there just a little longer, so my parents would be able to be with me even in spirit, just a few more days, and that was so heartening to me.

Back in Boston without my family seemed so different, so empty. I had a very difficult time concentrating on my work. But it was very helpful that I was able to squeeze in some business traveling to keep me going.

A month or so later here I picked up my family at Logan airport. As soon as we were in the car on our way home, the kids started to describe with vivid expressions, all the things they saw and did after my departure, including some mischievous acts they had performed. The one thing they had much fun with, I recall, was that a few times while they were in Kavouri, they managed to throw cats over the bathroom window to their cousins, Ceciliana and Katerina, causing an uproar to all around them! Additionally, they described the fun they had at the beach, and visiting some of the ancient mythological sights and old ruins. The worst disappointment for them was a private school which my parents suggested they should attend for a week, and that was a total disaster; they just could not wait to get out of that school. What a funny story!

The school year was now upon us and the winter weather started to show its undesirable face. Things were back to normal, and the routine style of our life was here. I continued to travel more and more covering practically the whole country, my favorite cities being Chicago, Kansas City, Louisville and Minneapolis.

It was on a particular day, when flying back from Chicago, that I experienced an incredible mental force. As I was looking over the clouds and thumbing through a LIFE magazine, my eyes fell on an article that hit me like nothing else before in my life. "DIVORCE: THE NEW AMERICAN TREND." That was the title of the article. I felt as if a magnetic force was drawing me towards that article. I was almost reluctant to put more attention to it, but I could not resist. Something was telling me, "You must find out what this is all about." Reluctantly, I started glancing through the pages quickly, having a hard time concentrating at the beginning. Curiously though, I found myself absorbed on the subject that in itself surprised me. Before I knew it, there I was, pouring all my efforts into that article, as if I was searching for water in a strange desert. The more I read, the more I wanted to know. My interest was creating a strange sensation, like "Why are you even looking at this report?" But I could not stop, and tried to find an answer to that, I just had to know more.

That essay was a serious, momentous turning point in my married life. Now, for the first time I began to question my Greek heritage. It perhaps had to move aside and I would have to accept the fact that I had no marriage. I had not had a marital relationship for over five years. The occasional affairs I had, (although discreet and away from home), were not only creating guilty feelings in me, but they made me think that my bond to my sons was the main reason I was still there with them. That alone was not good fathering. I needed to be not only a good provider but a strong, supportive, and disciplinary kind of father, and I realized I was not always that way. But those thoughts, almost immediately, turned to the way my Greek family would have responded to my situation. "Family comes first, and family tradition dictates, "UNION" at any cost."

As soon as I put that magazine away my head started to feel like it was hit with a baseball bat. I stretched back in my seat and I called the stewardess and asked her for a drink, and for the remainder of the two hours of flight all my thoughts were glued to one thing. Where am I going from here? Surprising enough the answer came to me much faster than even I would expect. "No matter what, I will promise my kids that I will be with them all the way, if they wanted me, until the time they are adults and out of high school." Furthermore, I concluded that, whatever I had read in that magazine, regarding DIVORCE, had nothing to do with me, "I am not ready for that, not now, anyway" I whispered to myself. That was my decision, good, bad, or indifferent and I had to live with that promise to my sons. However, to this day, I am not too sure that it was the best decision I made in their behalf, but maybe due to weakness in my part, or due to the Greek influence in me, I felt then that there was no other way I could have done it, and I could not find myself living without them, if the choice was mine.

# CHAPTER 8 – Looking Ahead in my Career

There I was now, back to my everyday activities, (routine as it may be called) and trying to make a living, while enjoying my life, the best I could.

However, as I had already predicted, and due to the nature of my specific profession, things in the chemical industry started to look more and more unsettled, and, to say the least, unpredictable for the foreseeable future, which kept me on my toes for many years to come. From here on I must concentrate, to some extent, on all the activities related to my association with the industry which I had chosen to be a part of, and which in essence, was a part of my everlasting adventurous nature.

By now it was evident that our company, being a division of a large conglomerate, had fallen into the same category as those suffering from strong competitive pressures and as a result the idea was formed that in a matter of time the company would, either be relocated or sold.

On a particular day around 1967, we were having an executive meeting. In that large conference room, seated next to the president of our company was a strange, large man, with a big belly. He started to explain to us some of the business's difficult situations. To me, the most significant statement made there was when he said, with a rather strong voice, "Now that the word is out that this division is for SALE, we are having so many offers; therefore, that alone makes me believe that you have something here worth saving, because obviously, it has

"VALUE". So let us all try to find ways to save this division", he said rather grimly.

From that day on it became evident that "THE SHIP WAS SINKING". One after another, people started to disappear, beginning with my boss, Dr. Perry, and then others. Even though I had some good foundation in the company and my job seemed secure, at least for the time being, I felt it was time for me to move on. My first thought was to return to California. I had an interview with the representative of my old job, in Chevron Chemicals, but it did not work out. But good luck was now on my side. One day, I flew to Chicago to attend the Annual Chemical Convention and, as I had previously arranged, I met there with the manager of a Chemical Company. After we discussed my prospects, he seemed interested in what I had to offer them and he asked me to stop by their headquarters in New Jersey for a more detailed interview, which I did, on my route to Boston. The interview went well and they offered me a position as head of technical service, at a better salary, and also they would allow me to commute to Boston during the weekends, until I found a home in New Jersey. I accepted it and there I was now in a new company. The job would be about the same type, much traveling, but a better equipped, more sophisticated and aggressive company.

After much searching, I found a beautiful, two-story, colonial home, under construction, with a huge lot, and many trees located next to what seemed like, a forest.

We put the house in Boston on the market and it was sold faster than expected. After almost two months of separate life style, we are all together again and enjoying this amazing home. It was not only huge, it had an enormous size basement, totally unfinished, which I thought some day I could convert into a game room, big enough for the kids to have all their friends over and entertain themselves, while being close to me, not somewhere unsupervised, and getting in trouble.

There we were, in a new location, new adventures, new schools, friends, church, and some new ideas on how to improve the situation with Mary Lou's way of life.The time had come for me to do more constructive thinking in reintroducing her into our family affairs, getting her more involved in our activities, and encouraging her to participate in our projects, since she somehow had allowed herself to be like a shadow, something like a ghost.

My first approach was that as often as I could, I would take her out more often, just the two of us, for dinner, a show, a night club or what have you. It seemed to have some positive effect, but not as much as I had hoped, but at any rate it was a start.

One of my wishes had been to put a swimming pool in the back yard, since I was able to finance it, and we had a large yard. It was something we all felt that we could do and enjoy it, including Mary Lou, since she was a good swimmer. Now after the swimming pool was completed we decided to build a basketball court next to the garage, and also a large cement patio connecting the pool to the rear door of the house. I ordered a cement pouring company to deliver the cement and the five of us, using pure muscle, with the help of shovels and rakes were able to do the job. I had never seen Mary Lou so energetic, so into doing something physical and she seemed to enjoy it. That was a good sign, I thought. Let's try something more.

It had occurred to me that one of the activities in which Mary Lou had expressed an interest was the use of potter's wheel to make all kinds of ceramics. I thought that would have some benefit on her and I made arrangements to have a huge, cement-type, kicking wheel, and an electric oven delivered and placed in our basement. At the beginning she showed a good deal of interest, but not a lasting one. So be it!

As the days and weeks went by I noticed that something was still missing in her life. The subject of her mother would come up and she would still show her usual anxiety. The boys constantly complained about her lack of interest in keeping up the house, "All she does is lay in bed reading, sleeping, and smoking," they would tell me as soon as I walked in the door after work. They started saying bad remarks to her, raising their voices to her, and that was something I would not allow. "Why, that is their mother they are talking to and about," was all I was thinking. No, this is no good! I never in my life treated my mother that way and I would never think of trying to; my father would have disowned me. On top of all, the boys were not doing too well in school; I had to go to the principal's office for conferences with him and John a few times. Steve was complaining that his mother was picking on him constantly. However, Eric was on better terms with her, but not always. There were times when I came home and found Mary Lou very upset complaining that the boys had been in a fight of some sort, and my reaction will be, "Go upstairs, all three of you, put your pants down and I will be there to belt you." I think that all I was trying to do was to build some discipline and be fair about it. That happened a few times and to this day, I can not tell for sure if it was a good idea on my part.

It was almost a year since we moved to New Jersey. Work was good, my health fortunately was good, and I did a lot of traveling. Overall things should be okay. But they were not. I felt I had to do something to find a possible solution to help Mary Lou. I searched around and found a good therapist in the area. For some reason I don't recall his name, but I remember that he specialized in marriage counseling and psychotherapy. I felt that was my last resort.

Our meeting was very cordial; he seemed very knowledgeable and confident that he would be able to help us. He asked Mary Lou and me a lot of questions and he insisted on talking to us several more times together. Then, after few meetings with both of us, he decided to have Mary Lou come to his classes with a group of other ladies. However, after attending some meetings, she became very irritable and asked me to join her in the next session with the doctor. "I was under the impression that we had a problem together. How come I am coming here alone and not with my husband?" she cried out obviously angry. To this day I can not forget the answer that doctor gave her: "Mrs. Mourelatos, I have asked you to be with a group of the other ladies alone because I believe this is the best way to help you, and when I think it is necessary for Mr. Mourelatos to join us I will ask him to do so, and I believe he will not have an objection to do that." For the first time in a long time I felt some relief. Somebody with some sort of knowledge and authority was giving me some credit. Now, after several months of this activity, and realizing that not much progress was made in our home I asked to see the doctor for an update. When I met with him he looked at me with a serious expression on his face and said: "Mr. Mourelatos, here is the situation, pure and simple. Your wife has no knowledge of her condition and she is not willing to find out. When she is in class with the other ladies her constant position is to tell all of them what they are doing wrong and what they have to do to improve their condition; in other words, she feels that there is nothing wrong with her, there is no need for her to improve, and she does not belong here." I was now in shock; I had to think fast. "What does this mean? Where do I go from here, doctor?" was all I was able to say. His response was, "You have two choices, one to continue with the program, and the other is to let her think of her own situation for a while and come back when she feels she needs some help. She seems to have an emotional problem derived from the bad relationship she had with her mother, but it is not very serious to the extent that she would require psychological therapy. However, group therapy will be helpful." I left his office with more questions in my mind than answers. I decided that the best thing to do was to keep it going for some time and see if there was any change, any progress.

Our life continued like this for some time. No improvement, no changes. About two months later she announced that the classes she was attending were a waste of time and decided to drop out, and that was it.

I was now concentrating on my work and trying to make sure that my boys got all the attention and guidance they needed so their lives would have minimum damage from all of the family problems they were now experiencing. That seemed to work well, I thought. Our house became a center of youth activities. They made so many good friends, and there was so much activity around our home, swimming, basketball, music, and of course motorcycles during the summer season, and skiing, skating, and tobogganing during the winter time.

One negative experience I had with John was, when one late afternoon I caught him smoking a cigarette behind the house. Later that evening I took him aside and stated in a serious voice. "Son, let me tell you, my father had a very serious problem, he almost lost his legs because he was smoking a lot, and I would not want you to get in the same situation, and hurt yourself. I just want you to think about it seriously, but if you decide to smoke, I want you to do it in front of me. I don't want you to think that you have to sneak around some place to do that". To this day I am not too sure if it was the best thing I ever did for John, since he not only decided to start smoking, he also encouraged Steve and Eric to follow his footsteps. Now I think maybe that was my mistake, I should have known better.

If only there was a way to convince Mary Lou that our whole family life would be so much more enjoyable and satisfactory, and if she could only try to participate in our way of life, and be with us, just as much as myself and the boys have tried to bring her in, that would have being so good! I was trying so hard to convince her that her mother was not a part of us and she should not allow her to destroy her life and our good family, but it seemed impossible to get through to her on that subject. For the life of me I could never understand how her mother, (any mother) could treat a daughter that way, and I expressed those feelings to Mary Lou. I was trying to convince her that she was basically a victim of her mother's past problems and behavior and she should be able to realize it and move on with her own life, because she was basically a good woman, and most important of all, she was the mother of my children and I would always love her for that and I thought she could have a happy life. That was something I tried many times, but I was not able to accomplish much.

# CHAPTER 9 – Visiting my Ailing Mother

It was now around the end of 1969 and about that time things at work started to look somewhat troublesome. I was rather heavily involved with product which, although it had received some good deal of acceptance in the marketplace it had some serious limitations. That product was a natural gum derivative of some sort and it had enjoyed good success in its use as a particle suspension agent, (a bodying agent) for many uses, mainly water based coatings. But this particular product was manufactured by others; all we were doing was to market it. However, that being the case we were having no control of the quality of its process and we ran into all kinds of problems and it ended up being removed from the market. So, I found myself out of a job, and although I was offered severance pay and stocks, it did not feel good.

It turned out however, that, my boss, being very well known in the Industry, introduced me to a large chemical company, about two miles up the street and I was offered a position there and started working in one week, not bad.

My assignment was very interesting and rather leisurely. I was what they called, Field Service Rep, promoting a product called titanium dioxide, a white powder used in paper, paint, plastics and automotive finishes, covering a certain geographic area around the Country. So, in essence, I was given a calendar with various assignments for the whole year, and I was to report to work, to the lab, only occasionally, whenever I needed to go there just to review some samples or pick up some displays. That came pretty handy. Now I was able to spend a lot of time at home and try to do what I had in mind all this time, in other words, to remodel the whole basement and convert it into a HUGE, game room. And that I did! Almost fifteen hundred square feet of play room, with pool table, ping-pong table, racing car tracks, pin-ball machine, stereo speakers, hidden lights, you name it. I never thought I would have the talent to do such a project, but I did it, and the boys loved it, and that kept them home, most of the time.

By now both John and Steve were old enough to be responsible for some of their expenses and started earning some money. John was working as a dishwasher in a Mexican restaurant and Steve was delivering local newspapers. Eric was enjoying the fact that he was the baby of the family. That was a unique era, however. It was the time that The Beatles would have almost total control of the air waves, both on the Radio and TV. The boys wore their hair very long, and the music would be played in very high decibels. But personally, I had no objection or concern about those activities. Besides, young people always fascinated me with their excitement, their energy, and their thirst for life.And now I had provided them with a game room and a place they needed to have fun, in our home, to entertain themselves, close to us, so they would not be out in some strange place and getting into trouble. That was my plan.

For some time now my mother's situation back home, had me very concerned. It started a few years ago, when; after she had a stroke she became an invalid and had to be moved around in a wheel-chair, a very painful experience for her and my father. I wanted so badly to go and visit them but I couldn't get around that. But one day, after I received an okay from work for an early vacation, I mentioned my desire to go and visit my parents. It was during dinner time when I told my wife and children my plan, but I couldn't afford to take the whole family along; yet, I didn't wish to go all by myself. Just before I was about to finish my thoughts, I received a good suggestion from John. "I would like to go with you as soon as you think you will be ready Dad!" he said to me, with a very positive tone in his voice. I just couldn't believe my ears. "Why son, that would be absolutely terrific," was all I could think to say to him. He really showed some strong interest to come with me, and almost immediately, I started to get ready for the trip. After some basic preparation with passports, tickets, etc. we were on our way to Greece.

What a beautiful experience! First of all, John by now was about fifteen years old, and he was such a handsome young man, tall, about five feet ten inches, his long blond hair waiving down to his shoulders, wearing a beautiful red velour jacket, that I got for him just for the trip, and that made him look so good. All those young ladies couldn't stop looking at him, both at Kennedy and Athens airport. When we arrived in Athens, my father was there to greet us and of course, to help out with passports, customs and all the necessary paper work. From there we went to their apartment where my mother was anxiously waiting for us. She seemed so thrilled to see us and with both tears and laughter, she expressed her usual kindness and warmth, while trying to cover her feelings about her handicap. Both John and I tried hard to avoid showing any pity for her sad condition, but I am not sure we did such a good job. She sure sensed it, but, she ignored it with her usual charm.

Before we arrived in Athens we were informed about what happened to the fabulous place of Kavouri. A few years ago, due to some political maneuvering, our house, along with a dozen other properties, was razed. That was so hard for me to accept. I could not really believe that I would not see that dream place ever again; it was just blown away with the wind!

The next day we drove to a nice two story house, which my sister, Rena, was renting for the summer, about a one hour drive from Athens, to this beautiful beach resort called Vraona. My mother, being in the wheel-chair, needed some help to get up those stairs and you could not believe the satisfaction John was showing helping to accommodate his Grandmother! That was such a pleasant sight. So there we were, father and son, in that strange place, sleeping in the same room downstairs, relaxing together, talking about so many things we never had the chance to do before, such as the way of life back home, the different life style the people in Greece have. Also we discussed some of the activities the young Americans spend their time on, like music, sports, and motorcycles and so on. We were having just a small talk. The next day we went fishing by the rocky part of that beautiful beach and it felt so good; that was just pure fun. The fish did not bite much, but the view of the ocean, the incredible smell of fresh air and that clear blue sky made everything feel so nice!

I never forget the way both my mother and my father were looking at John. They just didn't have enough of him and they treated him like he was someone super special. But I must say here that the most rewarding aspect for me was to see, once more, the beautiful way my father was treating my mother. There he was trying to put her to bed for an afternoon nap and he would caress her face, her legs, her thighs, kind of being fresh with her, and she would just gleam with a sneaking smile, showing her gentle approval. By looking at all that, my past experiences came back to life, the kind of LOVE and care from a husband to a wife that I was so familiar with, and which I was missing ever since my boys were infants. It all came back to me and I was feeling both happy and sad. It was also very important, I thought, that John had a chance to experience and see "IT" with his own eyes. Hopefully it would stay with him all his life.

Unfortunately my vacation was short, and before we knew it, we had to fly back to New Jersey. I was so thankful that John was able and willing to come with me on that trip; it made so much difference to me and I will never forget it.

We were now back home, and were trying to relive and talk about all those experiences we both had. John had a great time describing in detail what he had seen there and everybody, including his friends, were listening to him in awe.

The days and weeks were moving along and nothing special was happening except one evening, Mary Lou's aunt, Mary Clark, phoned her to inform her that her mother, Pauline, was very ill with leukemia. Of course we all agreed that she had no other choice except fly to California to be with her. In a few days she was on her way there. One week later she called to inform us that Pauline's case was terminal, and of course we explained to her that she should stay there with her for as long as it was necessary until the end of her case. We all agreed that this was the right thing to do and we understood how difficult and painful it must be for her. Pauline could not recover from her illness and three weeks latter she died.

After the funeral Mary Lou returned home, but there was something different about her behavior. She didn't seem sad, a normal reaction as one would suspect, but she seemed rather angry. I noticed that and I felt perhaps it was her way of showing sadness. But this situation continued and it was getting worse instead of better. After a while she was totally out of control. Obviously she could not handle the fact that her mother was not there any more and she had no one to blame for the way she was feeling about herself and the people around her.

Things were getting more difficult with lots of arguments. All I wanted to know was how the boys were taking all that was going on in our lives. One day I took them aside and discussed the situation we had with their mother. I told them that my concern was that in case I decided to divorce her, what their preference would be, either to stay with their mother or to come with me. I explained to them that whatever their decision was I would comply with it. It did not come as a surprise to me when Steve jumped to my question and told me, "Dad, we will go with you wherever you go", and at the same time John and Eric agreed as well. At least that was clear and now I had to figure out how to proceed. But this was not an easy situation, I had to really plan on it. My main thought was how my sons would do without a mother around, good, bad, or indifferent she was their mother. So I decided to let it ride for a while.

It was now 1971 and I received a notice that the company had problems with a lack of profits on the product we were promoting and had decided to eliminate the Field Service Department and the only thing they could offer me was a position at the Resins and Plastics Department in Connecticut. There it was again, just as I had predicted, being a part of unsettled, and subject to market adjustment conditions, I found myself in a position of having to face changes and new choices.

Well, I thought and thought about it and in the mean time I felt, since I had been enjoying the marketing type of activities so much, maybe I should consider going to direct sales. So I applied and I was offered a salesman's position for a chemical process equipment company located in New York City. But I was not too sure if that was what I wanted to do. In the mean time, I had accepted the offer to work in Connecticut. What a tough position to be in; I had to make a choice. There I was that particular morning, on my way to report for work in Connecticut, all the way from New Jersey, a one hour and fifteen minute drive, each way. The first order of business was to take a physical exam. Then I was sent to the Resins and Plastics Lab for orientation and then went for lunch with the rest of the staff. My mind started to spin. I was looking around like I was in some sort of uncomfortable chambers. I kept thinking, "Is this really what you want to do? It will be the same old type of activities, a different product, but the same routine. Besides it will be, even for a while, almost two and a half hours commuting to work. But what can I do? I have a family to take care off. What if I can't do direct sales? But they offered me a good job, I was well recommended from the other division and I was received here so well. But no, I cannot do this and I must decline the offer, and do it today". So after lunch I walked to the supervisor's office, the man who had hired me, and with an almost trembling voice I explained to him that "Although I would like to work here, it seems like the distance and the possibility that I would have to move, would be very difficult for me and my family to handle. Therefore I can not accept your offer to work here." He seemed, naturally, very surprised and very confused, but all he could do, like the good professional he was, he stood up, shook my hand, and with a very warm voice he wished me, "Good luck and a prosperous future". I shook his hand very firmly, trying no to look in his eyes, and I turned around and disappeared.

# CHAPTER 10 – My New Profession

New York, New York, here I come, ready or not, to do something "crazy", it seemed like. My office was downtown. I was given a car, decent salary, expense account and freedom of action. My territory was New York and New Jersey, calling mostly on paint and ink manufacturing companies. I was very familiar with the equipment I had to sell, but the actual mechanical function of them was new to me and I had to learn fast, and that I did. In fact, I received a welcome response from practically all the customers that I was calling on. "Nothing makes us feel better knowing that you understand what we need to do with your equipment Harry," most of them would tell me with a satisfactory tone in their voices.

Although the chemical processing equipment business was enjoying a good profit margin, in comparison to other products in the industry, the competition was fierce and companies had to look for ways to cut costs every step of the way. So after about a year working with them, and in spite of a good deal of progress we made in the market place, it was determined by the management of the company that it would be to their benefit, and less costly, if they would go back to the use of manufactory representatives instead of direct sales. And that was it for me. Now to start looking again for new possibilities.

The reality of my last experience was very beneficial for me. For the first time in my life I realized that not only could I sell but also

I was having a great time doing it. I really and truly enjoyed it! So, "Let's stay with that," I said to myself.

After some research, I found a good position, as a Regional Manager in New Jersey and the New York area, for a chemical process equipment company located in Los Angeles California. I rented an office only fifteen minutes from home, which was very convenient. As a matter of fact when Eric had to be hospitalized from an elbow infection, due to a basketball accident, we were able to have lunches together, bringing him what they used to call them "submarine". He sure loved the whole experience; we both have good memories of the incident.

Not only did I enjoy working so close to home, but business was also good and I was able to increase sales in the first year by 30%. Many times they would invite me to Los Angeles's headquarters for sales presentations and entertainment and all seemed to be going very well. Around the end of the second year I received an important call from the president of the company. "Harry, next week, I'll be on my way to Brussels and I would like to have lunch with you at Kennedy airport to discuss our program for next year." That was all I had to know. I met with him and in a very simple way he asked me to prepare a proposal for the upcoming national sales meeting in L.A., to show what I would need in order to make the following year a very successful one, sale wise, for the New York metropolitan area. After he explained his ideas, I asked him what amount of business he had in mind. He stated, very plainly, "One million dollars sales." and further he added: "Don't tell me now, just think about it and present your proposal at the sales meeting next month." Well, I thought this was quite a goal. When I took over the territory the total sales was about 55,000 dollars. In one year we had an increase to about 200,000 dollars sales. To jump from that to 1,000,000 dollars would have to be some aggressive plan but not an impossible plan, I thought.

A month later, there we were in this huge office. The president seated behind that large red oak desk, the CEO seated in a large leather chair, and on the opposite side, about ten regional managers were seated all around. After the routine introductions and some well meant expressions, the president, whose name I believe was Ed, started asking for next year's market projections of the various managers, from different parts of the country. To my incredible surprise all of them had an unrealistic and fictitious number to propose. I knew that it was not possible to achieve those objectives, because during the course of the year, we all talked and compared market trends and we knew what was accomplished and we had some basic ideas before we arrived at the sales meeting.

So, "Let's hear now about what to expect from the Big Apple", Ed asked with a very confidant tone in his voice, referring to me. I took a deep breath, knowing very well that what I was going to say would not be easily accepted, and I started. "I believe that 1,000,000 dollars for metropolitan New York is feasible, but let us not forget that I have three major and aggressive competitors in my area, who not only manufacture the machines locally, but they can deliver parts overnight, and, as we all know, the most painful and expensive experience for any manufacturing operation is a prolonged shutdown time. What I would need is a plant to produce machines and parts in my area and a show-room, so that I personally can demonstrate to my customers how to operate them".

There was all of sudden, total silence; no one was moving, reminiscent of funeral chambers. And then, Ed, with a surprised and nervous voice stated out loud. "But Harry, do you have any idea what your proposal will cost? Do you know how much each square foot of construction costs, then what would the maintenance, the insurance and the storage costs would be?" I was somewhat prepared for a reaction but not that vigorous. I had to think fast! So I started, "Well Ed, I must admit, I don't have the answer to your questions, but I must also admit that I am not as smart as you are, which is why I am just a regional manager and you are the president of the company, I repeat I am not that smart." As soon as I finished what I was saying, everyone was very quiet, no one said anything except the man in the corner, the CEO, who with a strong voice and obviously uncomfortable, shouted, "BULL S...!"

Needless to say, Ed was speechless. The meeting was over. No more comments. That sales meeting turned the corner. No much more was said, except Ed announced "Let's go to dinner now!"

On our way to the dinner the other managers stopped me to tell me, "You goddamned Greek, you must be out of your mind; do you know what you did in there? Ed will kill you!" "Yes, I know what I said, I told him the truth, but you guys, all of you lied to him, we all know that the numbers you gave him were totally inflated. You know that you could not possibly deliver what you suggested," I replied vigorously.

After that meeting everything changed for me, all the praises and the compliments I enjoyed receiving from the company in the past just vanished. I was one of the regular guys now.

It seemed inevitable that my future with that company would some day be limited if not restricted. I started to think about my alternatives. Many times in the past I had some thoughts about returning to California, but somehow by now I almost admitted to myself, if this venture falls apart I better think seriously about going back. Maybe it would be good for Mary Lou. My brother is back there, he is doing well, and I think it would be good for all of us.

By now we are around the end of 1974 and I was informed, (not much of a surprise), that the sales office would be closed, and a technician would represent the company, to do service work for all the customers in the area, and the company would be doing the sales operation by mail. That did it! I was out of a job and now I had to look ahead for something new. In other words, the adventures activities of my life are still in full force!

First order of business was to look for possible jobs in California. I started sending resumes to all kind of companies. After all, I had such a variety of experiences in all aspects of the chemical industry, that I thought I would try anything just to move back to California, but I wanted to have some sort of anchor in order to keep me going. I got a break. There was a good possibility for me to work in a paint company in Oakland as a Technical Director, but before I was to be hired I must have a personal interview with president of the company.

I called my brother in San Francisco and he suggested I should go and live with him while I was looking for a job. So there I was, right after Christmas, flying to California for a new life.

# CHAPTER 11 - Relocating to California

My interview went well. The president's only concern was that in spite of the fact that I had such "enormous" experience in the Industry, coming out of the sales aspect of the business could be a problem, but nevertheless I was hired.I started looking for a home to buy, and it did not take me long time to find a beautiful one in Clayton, about a half hour drive. We put the house in New Jersey on the market and it was sold in few weeks. The only sad thing was that I was not able to attend John's High School graduation. But anyway, he was the first one to come and be with me, taking a cross country bus ride, just to be here soon. I did not have any furniture yet, so he had to sleep on the floor. Steve and Eric followed, flying to Oakland, and bringing the cats with them. Then I flew to New Jersey to bring back Mary Lou, driving cross country in our station wagon.

We set up a household, with some old furniture some new. The idea seemed good at the beginning; the hope was that Mary Lou would find something here to be happy about. But the situation stayed the same. No much progress.

A few months later my job was terminated. I found a sales position for a pipe-line processing company, located in Tulsa, Oklahoma. I started traveling again which I enjoyed so much. Things looked good for a while.

It was now the middle of 1975, and I realized that Mary Lou was looking for a way out of the marriage, which surprised me. She talked to a lawyer and filed for legal separation. I was not too pleased with that idea, but I agreed to a divorce, and that was agreed upon, with the promise that she would find a place to move to. As per the settlement she would receive half of the equity of the house, the station wagon and her personal effects.

She was very reluctant to move out. However, one day I came home from work and she was not there; all three of my sons had packed her up, they put all her things in the station wagon and there she went. That was some relief, though not a pleasant one, it just had to be done. From that day on, the only person who had some contact with her was Eric, since he had some fair relationship with her. I am now living with my three sons, wondering what this entire situation means, where do we go from here, what are they going to be doing. Steve had graduated from High School in June; Eric had one more year to go. I convinced John to start Community College but that did not go far enough. Steve also attended College and Modeling School, which I thought was natural for him, but that lasted only a short time.

During this time of my life it was imperative for me to do some serious thinking about their future. I was concerned that the boys had it a bit too easy, not too much motivation, not looking far into their future. I started thinking that maybe it was my fault; I had to gently encourage them to be more self-reliant and more independent. The good thing was, in talking with John, I was able to reach him immediately. Before I knew it, he got together with some of his friends and rented a house in Pleasant Hill. Steve followed John's steps a few weeks after graduation. I started feeling that something is really working here. After Eric's graduation it was almost natural that he would go and move in with them. I was a bit disappointed though, since, after all my encouragement to get him into College, he did not try hard to do it. I always felt that Eric had the most brains in the family, but he did not have the drive. But now they are all together, and that felt good, I didn't have to feel that they were depending on me anymore, although I was close to them, and if they needed me I would be there in a minute. They started working and became men, and good ones. But the most paramount aspect here was that they were now together, and that was something I always felt very strongly about. It is based on the theory that one simple stick, no matter how resilient it is, can be broken with some forceful try, but three sticks, bonded together would be much more difficult to break. However, as I reflect now, this being year 2006, sadly, the bond I was hoping to build in them and expressed to them many times, lasted only a short time, (not necessarily that it fell apart), but as each one of them started their own families, that type of togetherness became less and less effective, especially after I moved far away from them.It is now around fall of 1976 and I felt that I had to start thinking of my future. I started feeling that my profession in the chemical industry was not any longer what I was cut out for. The most important and sad realization was that, in the corporate world, in order to succeed, you need to tell the management what they want to hear, worse yet, you have to lie to them, and that was not me. I needed some serious and radical changes. So, while still working I started attending seminars and training for the real estate business. Well I still remember the reaction of my attorney when I first mentioned to him about my interest in Real Estate. He shouted at me: "Harry, you are really crazy! With all that education and experience, you are giving it all up to do what a high school graduate can do? Let me tell you, I know a bunch of real estate brokers who committed suicide because they could not make it." But I had to try it.

My decision was made; all that adventurous activity with the Chemical Industry had to come to an end, after all those years, trying to find some stability in that field, was just not paying dividends. Maybe it was not meant to be or maybe that was not me, maybe I did not belong there, but somehow I had seen the reality of it, I opened my eyes and saw the TRUTH, and decided: NO MORE OF THE SAME!!!

And here is the beginning of new ventures. I was able to get my license and I started to work as an agent. After two years I got my broker's license and became a corporate broker owner not too long after that. My whole life had now turned around. Finally I was on the top of the world. For some reason I felt that this is what I was cut out for. I am a people person, I am up-front and honest and it paid off handsomely for me. I was totally independent and I was making good money. On top of that my social life was as good as it had ever been, and the most rewarding aspect was that, many times, some of the women I was dating, would tell me, in a nice way: "Harry, you obviously have so much love to give, how come you are still single?" My answer to that was always, "I have given to my sons all the love I could have given them, and I don't believe there is much more love left in me". But, in reality it came close, a few times, for me to get serious about some relationships, but due to my past experience, I felt rather scared about any commitments. Besides freedom seemed so much enjoyable, why spoil it!

We were at the end of 1980 and I felt the need to go and visit my mother and father, as well as my sister, who by now was living in Paris. So I flew to Greece and spent some time with my parents. It felt so good to be with them. My mother, still being in the wheel-chair, made my heart feel the pain she was going through, not been able to move around on her own and relying on my father for so many of her needs. That alone made me feel so sad. But it was so good to be with them. I hired a taxi and took them around to visit several places just so they would have some fun. At no time did I mention to them that I was not longer married, although they asked about Mary Lou. The funny thing was that while I was there, they treated me the way they always did, just like a child, their son, a fifty something year old son, and believe it or not, it felt good. But the time with them was too short, I had to leave, and had to say goodbye one more time, painfully so, and with tears purring out in my eyes as well as theirs. What a sad scene! On the way to the airport for my flight to Paris I had a strange feeling, "When am I going to see them again? What if something bad happened to my mother? How could my father survive without her? Maybe I should have stayed there a bit longer." Anyway, I felt good that at least I had the chance to be with them for a little while.

I had a great time in Paris with my sister and my brother in-law, Mike. What a guy! He was so successful at IBM, being a manager of Greek operations, that the only place to promote him to was in the International Division of Europe and he ended up in Paris. That was one of the concerns my father always had; he thought that transfer caused my mother to have a stroke. Since I left them first, then my brother followed me, and later my sister with her family moved to Paris. He thought it was hard for my mother to take that kind of break-up of our family. That was a terrible thought, but it was inevitable. At any rate, Mike and my sister were doing great. They were so happy to see me and at no time did they show me any concern about my being single. They showed me around to the most famous places in Paris, and all and all we had a great time. A few days later I flew back home.

# CHAPTER 12 - My Second Chance in Life

It was November of 1980, I don't remember the exact date but this was the day which changed my whole life. I was with my best friend and partner Vick in a night club, where I was a regular; we were having a rather good time dancing and having fun as usual. But there was not too much going on, not really. All of a sudden the front door of the club opened and there they were, three good looking women coming in; they seemed kind of different, one of them from a distance, looked like an Egyptian queen. She caught my attention. A few minutes later I approached the table where they were seated and started a conversation. To my surprise though, the lady who impressed me from a distance did not look as good close up, but then the other one attracted me a lot. It turned out that her name was Marta Alicia Palacio, and she was from Colombia. After a small chat I asked her if she would like to dance and she accepted rather willingly. We were dancing our way to heaven and before I knew it I felt something special about her. Vick and I, Marta Alicia and one of her friends, Maria Teresa, decided to go to my house for a drink. After a while Vick and Maria Teresa left, and Marta Alicia and I had a chance to get to know each other better. I was very impressed with her sharpness and her good manners. She was such a pretty woman, so worldly and so young. It turned out that she was twenty-two years younger than me and that got me little confused, I must say. What impressed me was that she was a very good and concerned mother. She was a widow whose husband had died from a massive heart attack when she was only twenty six years old, and she brought her two children to the United States to find a better life for them. She was living in Moraga, close to some of her friends, with her son Mauricio about ten years old, and her daughter Ana Maria eight years old. I believe what impressed her about me the most was my love for my sons and also my European background.

Meeting Marta Alicia was such a beautiful experience. I felt that I wanted to see her again and I invited her to my home for dinner the day after Thanksgiving, (for leftovers), which she accepted rather gracefully.

We had a chance to meet a few more times, but she mentioned that she had to fly back to Colombia with Ana Maria because she didn't like it here and in the mean time Mauricio would stay with a relative and maybe she would come back later. I thought that was it, except, a few days later I received a phone call that made all the difference, "Hi Harry, this is Marta Alicia. I am at the San Francisco Airport on my way to Colombia and I wanted to call and tell you that my last thoughts in San Francisco are of you, and I wanted to say goodbye." Wow! That made such an impression on me! "What a classy lady she is," I said to myself. I thanked her for her call and I wished her a safe trip and hoped to see her again. That was all I could say, still being in such a shock from the phone call.

I didn't know what more would happen with that adventure and I started wondering if I would ever see Marta Alicia again. But I did receive a Christmas card, and that was a good sign. Better yet, at the beginning of the year 1981, I got a letter from her stating that she was planning to fly back to San Francisco on February the fifth, to be exact, and she was wondering if I could possibly pick her up at the airport and take her to where her son lived with a relative. I responded by telling her that I would be very happy to do that.

Now, here starts the incredible story. It was now early afternoon, February the fifth; I was cleaning up around the house, just in case she would like to visit me. On my way to the airport, all kinds of thoughts were going though my mind; I am confused, what I am doing from now on, what does all of this means? But, for the life of me, I can not come with a clear answer.

The plane arrived a few minutes later than scheduled. I looked around the waiting room, just to see if there was a young boy about ten years old waiting for his Mother, but to my surprise there was none in sight. I thought that was so strange. Something must be wrong here, I murmured to myself. A few minutes later the passengers started to come out the gate, and there she was, Marta Alicia, looking rather aloof and excited, like she was about to go on stage. I ran to her and gave her a big hug and a big kiss and when I had a chance to pull myself together, I mentioned that something must be wrong because I didn't see Mauricio there. I think her answer was, "Maybe they couldn't make it". "I think you better come to my house for tonight," was all I was able to say, with some sneaky excitement in my mind, hoping she would agree to my proposal. And that she did!

On our way to my house, we stopped for dinner at a restaurant in Walnut Creek, by the name "LOVE", and after that we continued to the house. Now, no one would believe it, not even me, but Marta Alicia never left that house.

A couple of days later we drove to San Jose, so that Marta Alicia could visit Mauricio. I experienced something remarkable there. As we walked into her cousin's house, we saw Mauricio seated on the floor; the moment he saw his mother he got up, ran to her, grabbed her so hard and just like that, there they were, both of them on the floor, all excited, almost in tears, hugging and kissing each other. What a beautiful scene! "Now there it is, a perfect example of a TRUE mother", I said to myself. What a contrast from the way it was when my boys were growing up! But that was the way it was. Now is now. Since it was around the middle of the school season, Marta Alicia thought it would better for Mauricio to continue his schooling there and after the semester was completed we would bring him to a school close to us.

In the mean time I was going around wondering what would develop between us. The original thought was, since I was in Real Estate, I should be able to find a nice apartment for her, close by, so that we could see each other regularly. But after I did some searching, I came to the conclusion that the idea had no merit at all. Here I was, living all alone in this huge house and wanted to be able to share it with someone whom I was so fond of and had such a good time with. It would make sense only if that was what she wished to do. But, for some strange reason Marta Alicia seemed very comfortable living with me and before I knew it, she kind of settled in. That made a lot of sense, and as a matter of fact I liked it very much.

A couple of weeks went by, and this particular Sunday, while I was having an Open House for one of my listings, my boys decided to drop in to see me, and that was when they had the chance to meet Marta Alicia. It all turned out as expected. First, Marta Alicia was startled; John, with his serious and protective personality was wondering, "What does this mean?" Steve, with his outgoing attitude was all excited: "Wow, Dad; now that is quite a woman!" was his comment to me later on, and Eric, was not taking it too seriously.

Our routine was now very basic. Mauricio was traveling by bus to spend weekends with us. Marta Alicia started house keeping and we were having a marvelous time together. The more I was with her; the more I realized what a terrific woman she was. Besides the enormous love for her children, which had made a very strong impression on me, she was very intelligent and a person who spoke her mind. On the top of all that she was a very loving and sensuous woman, something that I had almost forgotten existed.

For some reason I wanted to introduce Marta Alicia to my brother, so we drove to Lake Tahoe to visit him and his wife Mary for a few days. Needles to say, both of them were very impressed with her, which made me feel really good.

I was now more and more into this relationship. I started feeling that I finally had been being given a second chance in life. I sensed that my fear of commitment started to disappear. I felt this was real, there was some seriousness in this relationship, and by no means, was it just lust. I saw a future here with a good woman. It was something totally different. - As I reflect now, this being the year 2006, I started wondering. Back in 1953, I was planning to come to America and of all places I picked up Moraga, California, as far as 9000 miles away. In 1980, maybe due to destiny or what is written in our stars, or what have you, I came in a relationship with a woman who came from Colombia, some 5000 miles away and landed in the same place, Moraga! How can anyone explain that? .... I came to realize then that I wanted something more, and that came about the right time.

Around June 1981 John announced that he and his girlfriend Jennifer were going to get married some time in September. The plan was that after church, the reception would be in my house. The question came up, "What about seating arrangements in church". Where will Mary Lou be seated, and where would Marta Alicia sit. It was John's desire to have Marta Alicia seated next to me, and his mother to decide where she wished to sit. Marta Alicia, gracefully, expressed no particular preference. So, I made a decision. I thought my best chance to ask Marta Alicia to marry me was now. And that I did. One evening I told her that I was really in love with her and wished to ask her to marry me. I did not have to try to convince her though; she accepted it and we set the date for August 14th.

We were married at the Ponderosa Ranch, near Lake Tahoe, in a very simple ceremony, with my brother, his wife and daughter Mina present.

It was now September 26th, John's wedding day. All went very well. We had the reception at our house, for about one hundred people. Mary Lou, her aunt and a cousin were present, and all seemed happy, including Mary Lou, especially after I had asked her to dance with me. That was a very good feeling all around.

Mauricio now lived with us and around the middle of December Marta Alicia's sister, Angela, flew from Colombia to bring Ana Maria to permanently live with us. What a strange feeling that was for me, to see this little girl, who had a very shy attitude, coming out of the gate and walking toward me. I did not think she remembered meeting me the year before. "For the first time in my life I will be a Father to a beautiful girl", I whispered to myself. That was quite a unique and warm feeling.

My first shock with Ana Maria came a week later when we walked with her to be registered at her new elementary school. After the routine introductions and registration, we started walking away from her and I must admit I felt so uncomfortable. "How can we do this to a little soul? What can she do there all by herself, in a strange classroom, hardly knowing any English?" That was all I was thinking in silence, not even trying to look back. I never expressed that to anybody, not even to Marta Alicia, I just kept it to myself. But all that concern was not really justified. Ana Maria turned out to be so smart, that within six months she was advancing so quickly that she surprised the school faculty with her progress, and before we could say how it happened, she was speaking perfect English. What a relief!

About a year later, Eric surprised us by announcing that he was getting married to his girlfriend Darcy. They decided to have a small and simple wedding. Marta Alicia and I both felt that it was too soon for them to get married but we felt that this is the way young people now days do things. So be it.

Steve, on the other hand, was very slow to make a commitment to his girlfriend Pam, and that was a good thing because they seemed to have too many arguments, which started to bother me a lot.

All seemed to fall into place now. I was a man with a new family. We had accomplished what is only read about in romance books. Happy together like it was supposed to be. My business was going good, we started to travel to Lake Tahoe, where the kids would enjoy some skiing and then to Colombia for me to meet Marta Alicia's family and for her kids to see the whole family again. I must say here that what impressed me the most about Colombia, besides her fantastic mountains, (which, by the way, are the most majestic mountains I have ever seen,) was the Colombian people. They are so much into family, so warm and friendly, full of life and outgoing. Basically it reminded me of my old Greek life style, my kind of people. I felt nostalgic about that, but that was okay. The best impression I experienced was Marta Alicia's father, don Arturo. He was a man loaded with wisdom, class, and humility. Although my Spanish was very limited we communicated pretty well. I was able to note almost immediately the love and affection he had for Marta Alicia, she obviously was his GIRL. Her mother, doña Ofelia, however, was a totally a different type of a person, kind of quiet, serious, stern and most controlling, reminiscent of the Victorian style of a woman. In other words, she was not a very loving person, but she was a very civilized and classy lady. All and all, Marta Alicia was born into a very special family, with four brothers and one sister, all of them doing very well and prosperous.

After visiting Medellin, (Marta Alicia's home town), we had a chance to take a short trip to that fantastic island of Hawaii. What a fabulous place! We really had a marvelous time together, just a fine honeymoon.

As the months started to pass by, our family started to grow closer and closer. John, Steve, and Eric became an integral part of us; more and more they got to appreciate Marta Alicia for her good qualities. As a matter of fact, Steve was so attached to her, and he started to call her "MOMMA", with a soft, nostalgic kind of expression, like trying to show that finally he found somebody close enough to him so he was able to use that word, something he obviously had missed all his life.

Now more and more our home became the center of activities, ever so often we would have all of them over the house for swim, basketball, croquet, dinners, the works. Everybody was having such a great time. The only problem was that we seldom were invited to their homes, and of course that did not seem too fair, but we kind of ignored it.

There was one concern in our family though. As Mauricio and Ana Maria were growing up we noticed that although Mauricio was adjusting to his new life, Ana Maria seemed to have some hard times and was making things very difficult for us. Many times we had to be firm with her so she would develop some kind of good perspective; however she was always at the top of her schooling, getting very good grades and she never had to be forced to study, which was a good sign. I still remember the times I took her for swimming lessons at one of the most famous swim centers in the country, The Heather Farms Swim Center. She would give me such a hard time, by trying to resist our efforts to keep her healthy and in good shape. What a brat!

It was now, I believe, 1985, and I received a terrible phone call from my brother. Our mother was in her last hours, and according to her doctor, she would be dead in a few days. So, I flew to Greece one day after my brother did. When I got to the Hospital room, she was in what seemed like, a comma, hardly breathing. As I am writing this now, I relive the picture of my father (after he asked everybody to step outside of her room for a moment), seeing him, through the small door window, kneeling on the floor, next to her bed, holding her hand, obviously praying and saying goodbye to her. What a beautiful and loving sight. How can anybody be so lucky to see this and feel that kind of LOVE!

After a while, the doctor came in and told us that it might take a little longer before she went to her eternal rest, and there was no need for my father or us to stay there. So we left. We had just finished dinner when we got a phone call and we were told that she just had passed on. The word was that she had waited long enough for me and all of us to be there before she was gone. Maybe that was true, maybe not, who knows, but it felt good to have been able to touch her while she was still warm.

The funeral was as impressive as it could possibly be. I stayed with my father for a few days, just to offer him some comfort. Fortunately, having such a large family, it was comforting that he would not be alone. So a few days later I flew back home. Not happy, but glad I was able to make it on time.

By now the grandchildren started to arrive. John now had Ryan, and then Eric had Michael, then Amanda, then Melissa. Then John had Tyler. Since I was in the Real Estate business, I was able to help John and Eric each to purchase a nice little house and also later on, to upgrade them, so they were now homeowners of beautiful homes. Steve's home came a little later.

I don't remember the particular date but I must say it really had a sad effect on me. I remember, however, that it was mid afternoon, and I received a phone call from Eric. He sounded very distressed. In a few seconds he was able to explain to me that he had just found his mother dead in her bedroom. What shocking news! It turned out that, since he was in touch with Mary Lou, from time to time, he had decided to give her a call, just to see how she was doing. Well, it turned out that for two days he was not able to get through to her, so he and Darcy traveled to her place in Napa, where she was working as a nurse, and Eric was faced with a horrible surprise; there she was, lying in bed, dead. According to the coroner's report, she had been dead for a few days, all alone in the house. It turned out that the gentleman she had been seeing from time to time, was no longer her companion. The funeral was arranged in a couple of days and all of us attended it. I must say it was very emotional. On my part, there I was, looking at the casket, which contained the remains of the first woman I ever really loved, the woman who was responsible for me to be able to establish myself in America, and who had given birth to my three sons. No matter how badly things turned out between us, she was a very important part of my whole life. And there she was laying, still, cold, in death, all by herself, like a neglected lamb, with nobody to give her some comfort, even at the time she was breathing her last breath, how sad. How can anybody, with any sort of emotions, witness such a tragic case, such an unusual trauma for a human being, without feeling a real pain, let alone somebody like me, who had so much to remember, such a connection with that person, thinking about her horrible life, and seeing her now lying there lifeless. But, hopefully now, she would find a true peace.

Eric had the strength and the will to make a very good speech, as a farewell to her, and that gave me some relief. Right after the funeral I took my sons aside and I said to them. "You must always remember that your mother was a good person, a gentle person, who, unfortunately had an unhappy childhood; she had never known LOVE, and although she had good feelings she did not know how to show them. Basically, I believe that your mother should have become a nun, she would have made a perfect one." I had thought so much about that and I came to believe it.

Around the summer of 1986 my brother made arrangements to have my father fly to San Francisco and we had a chance to visit with him for a few days. He was so impressed with Marta Alicia from the moment he saw her until the day he returned to Greece. She was, in turn, fascinated by him, with his charm and kindness. The two of them had such a way to communicate that was impossible for me to comprehend. She knew so well exactly what he wanted, such as for breakfast, and what have you. They would be able to "TALK" even though they did not speak the same language. I was so impressed one time, after I arrived home from work and as I was getting ready to jump into the pool, I looked out from the sliding door of my bedroom, and there they were, my father and Marta Alicia, sitting under the umbrella, talking, making gestures, and so on; I could not believe my eyes. Later, I was talking with my father, trying to explain to him some of the specifics of the neighborhood and his comments were

"Yes, I know about this or I know about that" and when I asked him how he knew all that, his answer was, "Marta Alicia told me!" Now, I said to myself, "How that can this be possible. She doesn't speak Greek and he doesn't speak English not Spanish". But sure enough they were able to understand each other! Other times when my sons came to visit my father, (while I was at work) they wanted to know more about him, and Marta Alicia was the "translator", back and forth. Go figure that out!

But the time is always the enemy when it comes to those situations and time does not allow us living through what we enjoy the most. A few days later he had to return to Greece and I will never forget it; I was hugging him in San Francisco, on his way to the airport, and I felt a strong desire to squeeze him so hard, like something was telling me that perhaps this would be the last time I would be with him. That very feeling turned out to be so unbelievably true. Only three months after his return to Greece, I received a call that my father had left this world.

My brother and I flew to Greece to attend his funeral. Since he was retired from the police, it was only fitting, to have a special police squad present, and that gave us a warm feeling, realizing that he was so well respected.

# CHAPTER 13 – Happy new life

It was now summer of 1987; I was doing so well in my business that I felt we should be able to take a rather long and deserving vacation. Marta Alicia and I invited her sister Angela, to join us and the kids to a whole month's trip to Greece. It was so reasonable, cost wise. My brother had an apartment available for our use, in downtown Athens, and a house in Egina, one small island close to Athens. My sister had a beautiful house in the Island of Kefalonia, a one hour flight from Athens and she had made arrangements for as to rent a place nearby for a few days.

It's hard for me to describe here all the exciting things which took place during that trip. All I can think now is that, one event after another, created such an impression on all of them. Marta Alicia for one, she could never have enough of the Old Athens, the Plaka. She has seen it so many times since then and her reaction is that it was the best part of all Greece. They all loved the ruins, the temples, the museums, and those beautiful Islands we visited.

Ana Maria and Mauricio felt that the Islands had so much excitement to offer them that they wanted to stay longer. As a matter of fact, Ana Maria, for the first time, was receiving some special freedom and privileges from both of us, which she really appreciated. Marta Alicia's sister, Angela, had a tremendous thrill about the whole thing. One particular event that sticks to my mind was when we all were attending a performance at the ancient theater, under the Acropolis. Angela, being single and a beautiful lady, was in heaven, not only from that incredible show under the moonlight, but from the fact that a handsome Greek man approached her and started to flirt with her. It didn't take too long for Angela to respond to his interest and the rest is history, and a good one, which seems like Angela has had a hard time forgetting. For Angela, Greece is the ultimate fun destination!

One of the trips we made was very special to me. With a group from the office we decided to rent a villa in Puerto Vallarta, Mexico. One of the memorable events there was the celebration of my 60th birthday. What a crazy time we all had over there. The thing that made the most impression on all was when Marta Alicia had a clever idea. She planned, a Mexican piñata, and the most fun which developed was, since there was no other way to blind-fold me, she improvised by taking off her bra, and using that. Wow, did that event create uproar! We really had a wonderful time that day, and in general, every day we stayed there, partying, dancing, swimming and so forth. While there, one particular event sticks to my mind. We were at this beach restaurant, having lunch, when all of a sudden, here comes a little boy, around eight years old, asking me if I would like to have my shoes shined.

The fact that I was wearing sandals did not make me wonder how to respond, I just started crying, and this little boy looked at me with wide, surprised eyes, especially since I reached in my wallet and took out a ten dollar bill and handed it to him. While I was drying my tears, and in a trembling voice, I whispered to him "No thank you". I am sure he never could understand that, while I was looking at him trying to shine shoes, my thoughts traveled so far back to Greece, when I was growing up and my father would point out to me an old shoe-shiner man, while lecturing me, "You see son, if you do not do good in school and study hard to become somebody, you will be just like him when you are older. Is this what you want?" And here I was now, in this fabulous place, having this poor boy bringing back to me those kinds of memories! How could I erase that thought from my mind, after all those years, in the presence of this little shoe-shiner boy?

Marta Alicia made a special effort to be a caring parent. I was always proud of that and very supportive of her busy schedule. She spent a great deal of time with Ana Maria's school activities, driving her around to various events and swim meets; and with Mauricio, who was so involved with soccer and delivering newspaper in the neighborhood. Both of us tried to attend as many soccer games as possible, and it was so much fun. I was always the loudest and annoying parent of all. We really never had any discipline problem with Mauricio, with the exception of one day when he got into an argument with Ana Maria. He got so mad at her that instead of hitting her, he punched the wall so hard that his fist went through it, opening a big hole in it. The next day, I instructed him that, since he had damaged the wall, it was his responsibility to fix it. There were no arguments from him, none whatsoever. I showed him how to repair it and he did it.

Steve and Pam finally decided to get married. They planned to get their wedding performed in a small, very charming Chapel in Lake Tahoe, during Memorial Day's weekend. They were a very handsome couple, very much in love. We had a nice dinner arranged for the whole wedding group, and I remember that it was so romantic, with beautiful trees surrounding their reception hall, and on top of it, some gentle snow flakes were coming down at the time they were off for their honeymoon! A year later they had their first child, Nicholas, and the second year, Felicia was born. All alone now, Steve and Pam seemed happy together. Steve was working very hard and advancing in his job as foreman for specially designed doors manufacturing company, in South San Francisco.

The same way that I helped John and Eric to get their first home, it was now Steve's turn. He bough a nice house in Martinez, about a twenty minutes drive from us.

# CHAPTER 14 – Family life

During the past few years, I was becoming somewhat concerned that something was going on under the surface of the families of all three of my sons. The worry was involving alcohol and in some cases drugs. That kind of problem started to disturb me a great deal. I, for one, was wondering how that could be possible. I have never, EVER, had any of that type of activity, and my sons knew that very well. The most I would ever enjoy was one or two drinks, and I never touched the other substances. I did not need to use them to be happy, but I never bragged about it. We had some discussions on that subject, but I did not make a big issue about it, (here again that might have been my mistake). They were now adults; that should be their choice, but why was this necessary? I was baffled about it. First, it turned out that Jennifer had a serious problem with alcohol to the extent that she needed treatment, and John went through some very difficult times trying to cope with that kind of adversity. We became aware that Jennifer had a very bad childhood also, and she had a very difficult time coping with that. But, thanks mostly to John's love, dedication, and support to her, as well as her determination to fight and win that battle, she was not only cured, but she is now a very successful employee at a medical facility in a managerial position. How about that for high achievement!

The other concern brewing was Steve's sporadic upsets with Pam. I had hoped that after they had gotten married and the children arrived, things would improve, but it did not seem like much progress was made. Steve was always open with me; he always showed much affection towards me and I felt if he had any serious problems I would be the first one to know. And he did that many times. There were occasions when he had some fights with Pam, he would come to us and talk about it and even spend some time with us. That had some benefits we thought, but something was very unsettling, and neither Marta Alicia nor I were able to pin point what the problem was.

One afternoon Marta Alicia received bad news from Colombia; her father was very ill with cancer of the lungs. She flew there in two days and stayed for some time. Unfortunately, no matter what the doctors were able to offer him, as medical assistance, it was not possible for him to overcome the inevitable. Marta Alicia tried so hard to give him encouragement to fight that horrible disease, but it had become too advanced, and finally, he went to sleep in her arms. They loved each other very much. By now, I'm totally convinced that the love of a father for a daughter is what makes a woman a great person, a good wife, and a good mother; and also the reverse I believe applies here, i.e. a bad relationship between a girl and her father almost always destroys the chances for happiness for her and the ones around her, and close to her.

At the very least, what she did, gave Marta Alicia some comfort; she was with him until his last breath was gone. She will always have some fond memories of her father, and justifiably so. He was such lovable, gentle human being. I have told Marta Alicia that he reminded me of my father in many respects, and that feeling stays with me to this day.

Slowly, slowly our life started to roll back to our normal style. The whole family was getting along very well. Some interesting things which developed come to mind. One day, on my birthday, Eric decided to surprise me. He came home and in a sneaky way, after he wished me HAPPY BIRTHDAY, he asked me to allow him to blindfold me, and took me out to the garage. Well, that was quite a surprise. There it was, seated in the driveway; a twelve-foot motor boat the family had bought for me. I was in total shock. All my life I wanted a boat more than any other toy, and they knew it. So here it was, one of my dreams come true! We used a few times and had great fun with it. Unfortunately, being that our house was far away from water we did not use it as we would have liked to, but it was fun.

Also, a couple of things which John decided to do for us were; first he took it upon himself to remodel our dining room. He knocked out the whole wall and connected it with the family room which made a lot of difference, and that was quite an improvement. Besides, at that time he was working for the Jacuzzi Company and he helped us in purchasing a big spa and he spent weeks installing it. The whole family had a chance to use it many times; we all had so much fun with it! After that John decided to go to College and receive his degree in Engineering.

As I see it now, this being 2006, I must say how much progress John has made in his career by working for a fine glass coating equipment company. They have recognized his ability, giving him many assignments, including various missions around the world, such as China, India, Hong Kong and Europe, where he installed and serviced highly sophisticated and complex equipment! He was always interested to know how things work and obviously made a career out of it, and a good one.

Eric was well established working many years for Pacific Gas and Electric Co. and all seemed well then. However, since PG&E made some changes, Eric had to find other ventures. He started to think about a more independent type of profession. After a few years of experimenting with Real Estate he became a responsible and strong Mortgage Broker. Now, after some marital problems with Darcy and eventual divorce, he decided to make a big jump in the Real Estate business. He was now the proud owner of his own company, having a number of agents working for him, making good money, and sitting on the top of the world! Who can ask for anything better!

Mauricio, after high school, went to Community College for a short time and then moved to San Jose State University to study Engineering. He was able to put himself through college by working and getting all kinds of student loans. Now that was quite an achievement! But his heart was always in becoming a pilot and right after his graduation from college he pursued his childhood dream, to become a pilot, which he was able to achieve later on.

In the mean time, Ana Maria, being so smart and such a good student, upon graduation from high school, with high honors, applied and was accepted at the University of California in Berkley. She managed to put herself through school, getting a degree in Political Science, working part time, and receiving all kinds of financial aid. What an achievement!

One very significant sign of Ana Maria's improvement and maturity became apparent a few years after her marriage. One afternoon, as I was seated in my room, all alone, (Marta Alicia was visiting her family in Colombia) the phone rang and as soon as I answered I heard Ana Maria's voice the way I had never heard it before. The tone of her voice was serious; she was nervous, and excited, all combined in one package. "I just wanted to call and tell you about something that has been on my mind for a long time" she started. "I feel that I owe you an apology for the way I treated you while I was growing up. I know now that you cared for me, but I just did not appreciate it as much I do now." I was lost. I did not know how to respond to that; it took me by surprise. I had to think fast, and all I was able to come up with was, "But sweetheart, you must understand that I'm also at fault because I never knew how to raise a girl. Since I raised John, Steve, and Eric, and then Mauricio came to me well before you did, maybe I didn't know how to treat you." Then she cried out with a strong voice as if I had said the wrong thing, trying very hard to correct me. "NO, NO, you had nothing to do with that, it was all my fault, my fault." I could tell she was in tears and almost simultaneously so was I.

The next day, I called her back to find out how she was feeling. Joe, her husband, answered the phone and almost immediately he explained to me that indeed she had been very upset for some time. She was planning to tell me what was on her mind but was not able to dot it. According to Joe, as soon as he came home from work, he noticed that something different had happened that day and she told him, "I DID it, I DID it! I called Harry and told him what had been on my mind for a long, long time and I feel much better".

From that very day on, my relationship with Ana Maria has made a hundred eighty degree turn. She is literally, the love of my life, and I am her DAD, no questions about it!

# CHAPTER 15 – My Retirement

So, there we were, Marta Alicia and I, in that large home all by ourselves, looking toward to our future together. We started thinking about some of the possibilities ahead of us. My work was doing well. My health, after some medical problems, (I had some very serious heart problems), had been taken care of, and I was now in good shape; so what will be our next step? It seemed though that Marta Alicia being home all alone, the kids going their separate ways, and she not having much to occupy herself with, was not too comfortable, and she felt that her life was too empty. The thought of her finding work was not my best choice, so the next best alternative was my retirement. And that was the decision and the best one we made.

The decision for me to retire, was not an easy one, I was very happy with my work, and the most difficult part was first, what to do next, and then, naturally, where? One of the prospects we seriously considered was Mexico. But the concerns of medical care and coverage were strong enough to negate that, although it seemed such a beautiful place to live. We thought of looking to Colombia and Costa Rica. But after traveling there and looking at all the possibilities we were not encouraged. However, during our searching for relocation, Naples, Florida, surfaced with positive and bright colors.

In April, 1992, after some very basic research, we felt the need to look closely at the city of Naples. We flew there and we were not only encouraged by its natural beauty, but also by the fact that the real estate values were so much more affordable, about one third of those in California. Economically, it seemed very much to our advantage to move there. Our next step was to make an offer on a beautiful condominium, put our house on the market, and move to Florida.

For some reason John and Jennifer showed a strong desire to purchase our house, so I was able to find a buyer for their house in Concord and made arrangements for them to be able to purchase ours.

A few weeks later, there we were flying to Naples, to our new nest. Mauricio and Ana Maria took time out and drove our two cars cross country and they flew back to California, after staying with us a couple of days.

The first order of business was to start furnish our condominium. Since we practically sold everything before we moved from California. That was not an easy task however. Ironically, the first major piece of furniture we purchased was my baby grand piano. Since I always loved to play piano and never had the time to spend doing it, I felt that now I would have the chance to devote time to it.

Within a few weeks we were all set having accomplished what we had in mind and were very pleased with the outcome.

After a while it became clear that I was benefiting the most from this move, since I was able to do all kinds of enjoyable things that I always had in mind, such as playing tennis, swimming, working out at the gym and practicing piano. Marta Alicia, on the other hand, started to enjoy the relatively small living quarters, having all brand new furnishings and a happy, easy community-life style to enjoy. Very quickly we made some nice friends and we became used to a more relaxed and comfortable life.

As the years started to roll by, our family started to increase in size. First Mauricio found the love of his life, Hope, and they decided to get married and reside in Seattle, where he worked as a pilot for Alaska Airlines flying all types of aircraft. They became the proud parents of four children, Lucas, Logan, and twins Hailey and Sabrina. Hope gave up her job at Microsoft to be stay-at-home mom and she is always busy with their kids. Ana Maria, on the other hand, married Joe and they live in Concord, California, and both are the proud parents to two beautiful boys, Patrick and Ryan. Joe owns his own electrical company and Ana Maria works from time to time using her good brains and mostly enjoying been a good mother.

It was around the middle of 1993, when I started receiving some bad news from Steve about his relationship with his wife Pam. At the beginning I thought maybe it was one of those family quarrels, something which happens to all couples from time to time. But it turned out that it was a lot more serious than I expected. One day, out of the clear blue sky, I received a call from Steve, and with a trembling voice he stated to me," Dad! Are you sitting down? I have some terrible news to tell you; Pam just left me!" That was such a painful, dramatic experience, both for Steve and myself. It all happened so fast I did not know how to respond to him, I knew they had some difficult times. I also knew that Steve had shown some emotional problems, and we discussed them many times, but I always believed in him. I always felt that the traumatic experiences he had gone through because of the way his mother had treated him were transitory, and with his enthusiastic and cheerful, and very kind personality he would be able to manage almost any hardship. But obviously I was wrong and maybe overlooked some deeper problems and issues which were disturbing Steve. Both Marta Alicia and I tried to comfort and encourage him to start building his new life, and with the strength and love he was receiving from his children and also from our love for him, he should be able to manage well and start looking forward to a new beginning.

Some time later they got divorced and both Pam and Steve shared custody of the kids. Pam later on remarried and Steve met Michelle some time after that. From the very beginning however, it became obvious that Steve's relationship with Michelle left a lot to be desired; she was a single parent of three children, one of them a young adult with bad behavioral problems, and the whole affair didn't seem to be a good choice. His problems started to surface almost immediately, but he was determined to try and make it work somehow (to my big concern,) so we had to let it ride. We kept in touch, but I remained anxious about Steve's situation.

For the most part, our life here in Naples was very relaxed and happy. We had a chance to travel to Greece a couple of times and several times to Colombia and all and all things were as good as retirement can offer. One of the most exiting things we did was taking our first cruise ever to the Caribbean Islands, Nassau, St. Thomas, and St. Marteen. It was that cruise, which was so imbedded in our mind that created almost an obsession for both of us to try some day, to do the impossible i.e. take a Cruise around the World, and that we did, back in 2001.

# CHAPTER 16 –
## Cruising Around the World

To even consider the idea that some day we would be able to take a trip around the World would, by all standards, be an unthinkable venture. But it became a reality, thanks mainly to our son, Mauricio. This was made possible to accomplish due to the fact that mostly all Airline Personal belong to Interline Travel Organization which enables them to obtain incredible travel benefits, including cruises, along with air fares, and those privileges are sometimes extended to parents. So, that being the case we were able to finance a seventy two day trip and here are the details:

On February of 2001, we sailed on Royal Princess from Ft. Lauderdale to Cartagena, Colombia, and spent half a day there, touring that fantastic city, which we had previously visited, and in my opinion it is one of the most beautiful and unique cities in the world; with so much natural beauty, incredible sea sides, unbelievable climate, fun place, and on top of that, great history from Spanish influence. From there we sailed through the Panama Canal. Now this is something one must go through to appreciate the incredible engineering and technological marvel. Just imagine standing on the front part of the ship, and only few yards ahead of you there it is a 70,000 tons ship, being raised by the mere power of thousands of gallons of water being forced upward on those devises called locks. Then, as that ship starts lowering itself, the liner you are standing on, at almost the same capacity, starts to lower itself by the very same process, REMARKABLE!

Our next stop was Manta, Ecuador. I was very impressed with the friendly and happy attitude of the people of that country. Although they seemed rather poor, you could read in them a very positive approach to their life style. Going through some shopping malls, it was impressive how well they presented themselves, and spoke good English, were well mannered and well dressed, even though it was a seaport.

Next we visited Lima, Peru. I, for one, must admit, was not too impressed, maybe because we did not spend enough time or for whatever other reason. But one negative aspect that stuck to my mind was the attitude of the locals; they seemed rather cold, suspicious and not friendly, not in comparison to Ecuadorians. But nevertheless, the magnificent architecture of Colonial Lima was notably impressive.

After Peru, we stopped at one of the most remote and mysterious islands, the Easter Island. The most impressive aspect of this island was those monolithic and rather non-artistic statues which obviously represented the simplistic life style of the natives, which still remains a mystery of how they arrived there and from where. The worst thing which happened to that unique island was the construction of a rather large airport that converted this remote island to a popular "tourist" spot.

We were now ready to enter the island that I had being dreaming about for years and years, the island of Tahiti. It was something else, not that I was disappointed, but for some reason I would not have minded, if, let us say, NOT THAT MUCH DEVELOPMENT and PROGRESS had been made. What a pity. What ever happened to those Polynesian beauties, running around in their grass skirts and bare breasts?  In order to see them you must attend a special show, which we did, and that was fine with me; but I felt even that had a limited appeal. It did not have the natural aspect of it. Simply put it was a commercial act, not bad, but not the real thing. Fabulous water falls, about thousand feet high, with fantastic greenery and millions of beautiful flowers made up the difference. However, the black sand was not to my taste, since I was always a (sparkling- white-sand, kind of a guy) but so be it.

Our next stop was American Samoa Island, Pago Pago. Here, we found a lot more natural beauty than in any other of the Pacific Islands we had visited so far. From my perspective, Samoa had a lot more exotic appeal and more tropical outlook, and in reality, a more layback life style. The natives were obviously happy people. It was a very pleasurable experience, just looking at them! However one significantly interesting and unique feature were the tombs of all their family's members, placed in front of their homes. What an unusual and novel display of affection.

As we approached New Zealand, we realized that, besides its larger size, in comparison to the ones we had just visited, we were looking at huge mountains, so bold and so steep as if they are rushing down fast to meet the sea. The main characteristic of this beautiful island is the ever-green color all around, and the enormous amount of roaming sheep we saw while traveling from Tauranga in the Bay of Plenty to the city of Auckland. As you travel around, you find yourself surrounded with all kinds of geysers, steamy phenomena, which becomes obvious that somehow, somewhere, thousands of miles below the surface of the earth, some type of water, run into a very hot lava, which was converted to steam, and for some strange reason it found a weak earth crust in that particular location and broke through it. But the highlights here are the flightless birds which New Zealand proudly claims as unique property of theirs, and those are the kiwi and kakapo, which being nocturnal can only be seen in captivity. We also found out that New Zealand is very peaceful country, as it was manifested by the lack of policemen and police stations (if you could find one.) The attitude and the friendliness of its people was such an overwhelming and very refreshing experience one can hardly forget.

It was now around the beginning of March 2001 and we were sailing towards the incredible Australia. As if it was just yesterday I still remember that morning coming in to the Sydney Harbor. It was about six thirty in the morning, a beautiful sunrise under clear skies, and here it was in front of us, (as we were standing in the bridge area of the ship,) the huge and famous Sydney Bridge, and the ever impressive and majestic silhouette of the Opera House. What a sight! Well, I for one had a good feeling about visiting Australia but I had no idea I would be so impressed with that country. It was not only the climate, the beautiful  beaches, the surfers, the zoo, the people, the 2000 Olympic facilities and the mountains, but the whole thing about Australia which makes one think; where on earth is there a better place to spend the rest of your life?. And if that was not enough, we were traveling now to the ultimate place, that paradise called HAMILTON ISLAND. My God, if there is anything more beautiful place than that place, I would like somebody to direct me to it.  No wonder George Harrison, the very famous Beatles singer, was lucky enough to build a fantastic mansion there. He obviously had good taste for the best of everything.

After such a fabulous experience, we did not know how we could top that, but it turned out that Manila, Philippines, had some good points to offer. One of the most impressive places was the American Cemetery. That was a very significant sight to see. I don't know for sure but I believe it is the largest cemetery in the world. Filipinos are a unique race, having been exposed to many cultures and historical events, such as Chinese occupation, Spanish rule, German occupation, and finally receiving their independence from United States in 1946. But they seemed to be the type of people that have some unique worldliness about them. They are friendly, very accommodating, and willing to serve others without any hesitation. Although it is not a rich country it has a very fertile climate, which offers good bases for growth on agricultural products.

Now we were in for a big surprise. We had heard so much about Hong Kong, our next destination, but we had no idea that it would be such a shock. Beginning with the size of it, such a small island, one would not believe the enormous progress they have made in recent years.

On Aberdeen Village you are faced with house-boats and the "sampans". Those are small and unique boats; most of them been used as local transportation and as a tourist attraction. Then they have the "junk" boats that are colorful and huge floating restaurants. Next you see lined up along the bay thousands of high sky-scrapers one built next to the other almost touching each other, like a continued fence. Its uniqueness is based almost on the fact that this small country, the size of about six million population, all squeezed in an area of 413 square miles is one of the world's foremost centers for trade and finance and this capitalistic enclave is now under the communist China domain. As we moved about visiting various sites, the outstanding impression one got is the enormous technological advances abound, the wealth of goods and merchandise and the high level of education that is obviously dominant among its people. Due to the fact that the land is obviously at premium, it is most amazing how they manage to build those high-rises at the side of the hill with no concern of land slippage at all. They must have found the secret of good ground support, was all I could think of from my perspective. Now I believed all I had heard about this fabulous place, Hong Kong, the wonder land!

We were now on our way to visit a significantly different country, Vietnam. We had no idea what to expect but sure enough we were in for a surprise, a positive one for that matter. Ho Chi Minh City, the capital of Vietnam, was something we did not expect to be so impressive, not necessarily from its physical form, but from its people. For whatever reason, we found its people to be the friendliest, the most accommodating and amazingly so, the happiest of what we had been seeing in other parts of the world. If their smiles were not real we would never know it, but it was there. One would admit that by the appearance of things, Vietnam was very poor, maybe one of the poorest countries of the world. The main means of transportation were the bicycles, motorcycles and some beat-up cars and rundown buses. The ones we enjoyed the most were three-wheel bicycles, at a small cost for a ride around few blocks (for a token cost of one dollar). Imaging that, the tip was "higher' than that. One very unusual and unique entertainment we had was the water-puppet show. We thought that not only was fun watching it, but also the technology they used was totally amazing and very new to us.

As an added and unusual luck we were able to see a Funeral and a Wedding Parade the same day. But interestingly enough their folklore tale states that, "if you see a funeral parade it is considered  GOOD LUCK, but if you see a wedding parade it is considered BAD LUCK." So now the question for us, since we had seeing both, "Where are we standing on that?" Ha-Ha.

If one could only imagine what that country had to go through over the hundreds of years of its existence it would become clear the reason of its sad state of affairs. All those conquerors, such as the French, the Chinese, the Japanese, and then the latest Vietnam War with the United States had left that county with not much to build on, but, for some reason they seemed proud enough to want to stand up and make something of themselves. One positive note is that they realize now the benefits of good education and they have established financial support for schooling, and education is free! Now, how is that for looking forward?

Our next stop is to the country that has the reputation of being the cleanest place on earth, Singapore. It is something very unusual, I am sure, just to think that, coming from Vietnam to visit Singapore it is like changing clothes from jeans to tuxedo. And to think that this is one of the smallest countries of the world, with a population of around three million people all crowded in an area of 221 square miles! It is really remarkable how they have become so prosperous and have world-wide connections with major industrialized countries with petrochemicals, textiles, and shipbuilding facilities, as well as banking and financing. The aspect of being a clean country becomes evident the moment you step in it. It has been said that if you are caught dropping a cigarette butt on the street you will be fined heavily. But really, all you have to do is just go through a shopping mall and you will realize how spotless that place is! You must question, just by looking around you, how they have managed to set up such high standards regarding cleanliness! Everything around you is not just clean, it is shining clean; you can literally eat from the floor. The streets are totally washed clean, bushes and trees are trimmed, flowers blooming and pavements and side walks are well maintained. Now that is a CLEAN CITY!

We are now in a very complex place, the city of Kuala Lumpur, Malaysia. It is a much larger country with a population of about eighteen million people with a very interesting history and many cultures and religious affiliations i.e. Muslims, Buddhist, Hindu and Christians.

Malaysia, in spite of all its numerous historical problems with occupiers and conquerors, such us the Chinese, the Portuguese, the Dutch, the British and the communists, is considered today one of the richest countries in that region. Its wealth is notably from the good use of large number of rivers, its fertile climate, its good production of wood and metals and of course its petroleum products.

One of the most impressive spots we visited was the Palace of the Sultan Sehecai Kain. From what we saw by the gate, (not being able to go in), it was just a fantastic, luxurious and incredibly rich looking place. The other aspect which is worth noting here were those fabulous looking gardens abound. The people seemed very worldly and very outgoing. We also noted some areas which seemed rather oppressed and poor. Their strong religious beliefs, mostly Muslims, are manifested by their social life style. It was highlighted to us that if a couple is caught "fooling around" in a public place, they would go to jail. All and all, that was a very unique country.

We were now traveling west on the Indian Ocean. Our next destination was Cochin, India. We arrived at the port early in the morning, and we traveled by bus (as it seemed for a long time,) and finally we arrived at the heart of Cochin. Now here it is; a place totally in a category of its own. By all appearances it must be the most neglected town I have ever seen in my life. As we rode our bus through the town we were faced with a sight of pure poverty. Dirty and poorly paved roads, small homes looking like they are in need for much repair, stranded cows roaming freely on the streets, people walking around bare footed, right next to, what looks like, a contaminated water running creek, and children walking slowly crossing the streets like there is no need to rush into anything. The main means of transportation were bicycles, motorcycles, and beat-up cars. Going close to the fisherman's center you will find the most unique and ingenious contraption of fishing apparatus made of a number of wood poles and fishing nets that really inspires your imagination, very primitive,  but very effective.

I came to think that Mahatma Gandhi visualized the conditions his people did have, and that alone inspired him to devote all his life and energy to making sure that kind of life style needed an effort and dedication by someone, so that it would be improved for ever.

After we had spent some time visiting Cochin we shipped  north and arrived  to a totally different city of India, the city of Bombay, or what is now being called Mumbai. Immediately, you feel the difference as you arrive here. To begin with one realizes that this country is part of a civilization which is traced back to 2500 BC, and has gone through a number of conquerors, (which created cultural and occupational changes), such as Mauryan, Turkish, Mongolian and British, until it received its independence as late as 1950. The very fact that India's population has now exploded to almost one billion people, was manifested by what we were able to observe going through in the city of Mumbai.  Neither I nor any of our co-travelers had ever seen such an enormous amount of people, all packed together in one city. The congestion, the noise, the traffic, the pollution, the crowded streets, the huge amount of buildings, one next to the other, was something totally out of reality.

I must highlight here that what made the most impression on all of us was our visit to the public laundry center. I don't think there is such a place in any other part of the world. Just imagine, you are now looking in an area the size of, let's say, a large football park, and all you can see is an enormous crowd of people, men only, standing in front of tubs filled with dirty water, beating the dirt out of the clothes and spreading them on the rocks to dry after being rinsed in that brown water. That whole thing was so strange!

It seems that India, has made an enormous effort to educate its people and it has been manifested by the fact that they now claim to have a large reservoir of highly educated workers, many of whom are now working overseas. It is well known now that India is a major industrialized nation with all types of power including nuclear.

It must be said here that our trip to India was not only informative but something that kept your mind wondering, what the world can expect from such an enormous amount of people that have developed such educational advantages; what indeed would they do with all that mental force, and how will they be able to squelch their thirst for more knowledge?

We were now traveling toward the Arabian Peninsula.Our next stop is Salalah, Oman. The moment you put your foot on that country you know that you are in a different world; nothing but sand, desert, goats and camels. People wearing nothing but white robes and turbans, just to keep themselves cool. But there is a good sense of confidence and pride in those people, and there is a good reason for it. Having to go through years of unsettling military and political upheavals, and overcoming warring Arabs, Portuguese and British rulers, Oman became an independent nation in 1971 and established a successful Monarchy. The main religion here is Muslim and the language is Arabic.

Fishery and petroleum products have become the core of its economy and they are enjoying a very peaceful life style. One of the most exciting products we were introduced to was the very unique tree called Frankincense, which is famous for its production of spicy products. The most notable style of housings there were those huge buildings, looking much like condominiums, which in effect are nothing more than family homes, and are occupied by all kinds of family members, such as, parents, children, grandparents, uncles, aunts, and so forth.

Some people say that you always leave the best things for last. If that is true, we were in for a fantastic experience, more than we ever expected.

After we left the port of Salalah we sailed westwards to one of the most fascinating waterways of the world: the Suez Canal. There are no easy ways to express the impression one gets while traveling through those waters. To begin with, the idea that it takes twelve hours to cross this canal is almost overwhelming, and it is not its length but the slow allowable speed that must be under control.

The very idea that we were able to visit some of the most historic, ancient places in the world, such as the ruins of Luxor, the Valley of the Kings, the Sphinx, the Pharaoh Palace, the Pyramids and so many well known places, which have been there for people to marvel for almost five thousand years, goes beyond the human imagination. The Egyptian history has so much to offer to the modern world that one can only truly appreciate by taking the time and step on those grounds and see first hand what civilization was all about. I, for one, was so impressed standing in front of the Pyramids and trying to assess the enormity of effort of the Egyptian workers to be able to build that fantastically enormous structure. Then I started thinking, okay, I can see how the workers, the slaves and others were able to, with ropes and sand and what have you, place the first, and then the second, and even the third heavy stones, (the size of an average automobile) one on the top of the other, but to be able to keep building that structure to a higher level, as high as hundred thirty feet, using those primitive means, was something my limited brain power could not possibly conceive.

The realization that we were indeed in Egypt and in front of the Pyramids came to life when my wife Marta Alicia and I took a ride in one of those huge and well decorated Camels, barely being able to stay on it, without falling off, and we realized that we could only do that by holding close to one another, a crazy and interesting experience, but painful.

Yes, I must admit, that as long as I live, I will always consider the Egyptian ruins as one of the most impressive sites I can think of.

After we left Egypt we sailed toward the Mediterranean Sea and arrived at the port of Kusadasi, Turkey.

The town of Kusadasi and specifically the ruins of the historic Ephesus were one of the best surprises of our trip. It was so hard for me to believe the progress the Turkish people have made the last few years, their organization, their appearance, their good English and their professional attitude were amazing.

Ephesus ruins, represented a classic Greek culture, in combination with some Roman history, and produced a good deal of interest. Looking at the amphitheater which had the capacity of twenty four thousand people seemed almost unbelievable, considering that it was built so many thousands of years ago. The remarkable aspect of the public library, being built next to the houses of ill repute, and close to the open air restrooms, was something of great interest and real amusement, to say the least. However, although I am not a very religious person, our touring the "House of the Virgin Mary" took me by surprise and I felt very emotional and I could not hold my tears from flowing to my cheeks. That was some experience and hard for me to forget.

So, after seventy days of cruising with the Royal Princess covering five continents we sailed to Athens, Greece, which allowed Marta Alicia and me the chance to see my country one more time.

We arrived in Athens, I believe it was April 26, 2001 early morning, and we spent a day at my brother's apartment in downtown Athens and from there we flew to the Island of Kefallonia, to spend few days with my sister, Rena, in her fantastic house. There we were joined by my brother and his wife Mary, and all of us had a great time together, visiting, having fun, and as a matter of fact we were able to celebrate my seventy fifth birthday together. We had such a wonderful time, after being separated for so many years; and now there we were in this beautiful Island, entertaining ourselves in that marvelous beach, and spoiling our taste with Greek food in those romantic restaurants right by the water. What a wonderful experience!

After two weeks together, we flew to Athens and from there to Frankfurt, Germany, and then home to Naples.

# CHAPTER 17 –
## Second Cruise Around the World

After our very long trip what we really needed was to rest and try to put our life back to normal.

We had a chance to travel to California and Seattle to visit the children and grandchildren and that was the extent of our traveling for the remainder of the year.

Sometimes the agonies of life come at the most unexpected times. There we were, Marta Alicia and I, settling back happily, reminiscing about all the wonderful moments we spent together, traveling to those fantastic places around the world and just simply feeling good!

By now Steve started to have some problems in his life, and most of them were related to his new relationship: Michelle. At the beginning they seemed to be minor problems and I, for one, tried to discourage Steve from getting more involved or too serious with her. He seemed to agree with me at the beginning, but for some reason he felt he would be better off being with her, and soon after that they got married.

Not too long after their marriage, and after they purchased a larger house to move into, they started working together at the same company where Steve was employed for many years.

By now it became evident that things were not working too well for them. In spite of Steve's efforts to be a good father to her children, there was a big gap among all of them, and their relationship started to deteriorate. Steve was determined to make it work against all odds. He and I had a lot of discussions on the subject for many months without a good outcome. So we let it ride.

It is now the middle of 2002, and we were having Marta Alicia's nephew, Augusto, living with us while going to college. He is a very nice, soft spoken young man, and always a pleasure to be around. In the mean time, Angela and her husband Fausto, came from Colombia to visit us for a few days. It was during their visit here, on April 18th, that we received the bad news that their mother, doña Ofelia, had just died after a short illness, at the age of eighty five. Needless to say, the news were very upsetting to all.

It was now around the beginning of 2003, and we received good news about the possibility of taking another long cruise around the African Continent. How exciting!!

So, after all the preparations were taken care of, there we were, Marta Alicia and I, flying to Tokyo, on our way to Singapore in order to catch our ship, the Norwegian Crown, and sail to some fantastic wonders of the World.

Being in Singapore for the second time, only just two years ago, we felt that all seemed so familiar and just as impressive as it was the first time, nice, clean, rich, peaceful and friendly country. From there we again had to visit Kuala Lumpur, Malaysia on our way to Phuket, Thailand.

Phuket did not make much impression on us, not nearly as exciting as Vietnam. The only thing I have for a memory from there was when we stopped in one of the vendors stands and I was convinced that I had a good chance to buy a ROLEX, which I did, for the price of eighteen dollars, not the real thing, but almost identical, Ha-Ha.

From Thailand we sailed to Colombo, Sri Lanka. Now that was something which is almost impossible to forget. The people seemed rather poor but you can see in their eyes the will to live and do things. They crowded those stores and moved around in groves and with purpose. The most impressive spot was the elephant village, a refuge, where hundreds of elephants were roaming around, playing, fighting, taking a bath and what have you. It was such a fascinating sight to see, those huge animals acting like children and making strange moves and funny noises.

From Sri Lanka we sailed to India. We revisited Cochin and Mumbai, but this time we had a chance to visit Goa. It seemed no much different than Cochin.

From India we had a chance to visit all those incredible islands of the Indian Ocean: the Maldives, the Seychelles, Mauritius and Reunion. All of them had beautiful beaches, incredibly  clear blue waters, pure white sand, just as good,  if not more attractive than those of the Pacific Ocean. - As I am writing now, this being year 2006, I recall the terrible destruction, those islands suffered during that horrible Tsunami of 2005. It seems almost impossible to imagine that those exotic islands had suffered so much from that destructive force, and that thousands of people perished because of it. -What a shame!

We were now sailing around Madagascar and arriving at Richards Bay, South Africa. From there we took a bus ride to the  famous Kruger National Park, one of the country's best game reserves, and we had the most fantastic experiences one hopes to have before their life is ended, a SAFARI. Riding on those special safari jeeps, we were able to see beautiful, wild animals, roaming free, in a fantastic and open environment. Although we did not see what I wanted to see most, the lions, we saw almost every thing else, such as giraffes, zebras, antelopes, leopards, rhinoceroses, hippopotamuses, baboons, buffalos, gnus, and impalas. I was in a total awe. All my life I had been thinking, what it would be like to ever have the opportunity to have this kind of experience, to see the real life of a wild kingdom. What a thrill! "I must be dreaming", was all I could think! From there we sailed to the port of Durban and had a chance to visit another park where ostriches and wildebeest were roaming freely. Also we had the opportunity to visit a truly unique place, a Zulu Village. Imagine that! Real people living in a totally primitive world, spending their whole life in straw huts, wearing their unusual customary outfits, and working on various types of crafts. You see women going around with their beaded skirts, bare breasted, and the witch "DOCTOR", hardly wearing any clothes, smoking his favorite, LEGAL, marijuana pipe! From there we sailed to one of the most famous place of Africa, the Cape Town of South Africa.

This is a country with a wealth of history and different cultures, which for over hundreds of years went through occupants and settlers such as Portuguese, Dutch, Germans and British, and finally in 1961 it seceded from the British Commonwealth and became a Republic.

One of the most famous spots, worth seeing, was the prison where Nelson Mandela spent 27 years, due to political differences. It is now a well known fact that, after his release from prison, he brought dramatic changes in their government and that country now breathes fresh and free air. Just seeing that prison, from a distance, makes one feel the impact of the historical effects of his efforts in order to save his country.

Today, as we viewed Cape Town we realized how vibrant, how advanced that city is. People seemed to be so much into a move-on, progressive, intelligent and cosmopolitan way of life.

One of the most fascinating sights, one should never miss, is the famous Table Mountain. It was not only its natural shape, a totally flat top mountain (the size of a small town), but also the incredible technological marvel; the cable cars, (which were so well designed and so well performing,) it enabled the public to go up there and comfortably view that natural wonder. As we arrived there, it was apparent that one felt as though you were in a flight pattern, totally surrounded by clouds, hardly being able to see the Cape Town beneath you. What a magnificent view!

All and all, that was one of the most memorable countries we had visited, worth visiting again and again.

We were now on our way to Walvis Bay, Namibia. This is one of the African countries which produce many types of minerals, such as diamonds, gold, copper, lead and uranium dioxide. The climate is almost always dry. One of the most impressive things we saw was the many mountains of sea salt beds and sand dunes. It was really unbelievable. But just as impressive were those thousands of white flamingoes roaming around the beaches of the beautiful Atlantic Ocean.

Next visit was at one of the most remote and isolated Islands we had ever visited, the Cape Verde Islands, somewhat neglected, and obviously a poor place. This is considered one of the smallest countries in the world that obtained its independence from Portugal as late as 1975.

We were now sailing towards Canary Islands; it took four full days of sailing to get there. During that long trip, there was not much to do. I was invited by the cruise director to participate in the passenger's talent show, and since I am such a ham, I did it, playing piano for them. Now I have a T-shirt to show for it. Well, that wasn't too bad!

Canary Islands, their name taken from their native wild canaries, are by far one of the most attractive islands in the world. The islands were originally controlled by the Spaniards but by the year 1341 the Portuguese took over their ownership. The main attraction of the islands, besides their natural beauty, is the abundance of birds and wild animals, the flowers, and to some extent the extinct volcanoes.It is worth noting here that the chief source of revenues for that country is the year-round visitors, followed by its agricultural products.

Our next stop was Madeira Island. An absolutely beautiful place! We were having such a good time with the locals, tasting their famous local green wine, that we almost missed the boat, to the anguish of our cruise friends who were desperate, hearing our names over the speakers, and knowing we were the only passengers not yet aboard. Now that was scary!

We were now at the final destination of our cruise; that is Lisbon, Portugal. What a fantastic city that was. Totally European, almost immediately reminded me of Greece, my world. Such fabulous architecture, an old but classic city, so many castles, old palaces, many ruins and so on and so forth. The way people looked and acted was so familiar to my kind of people; outgoing, happy, musical.

Marta Alicia and I remembered our special treat there, very vividly. Since we were going to spent a few days in Portugal, we decided to splurge a bit and we hired a limousine, a Mercedes Benz, to be exact, and were very fortunate to find a chauffer who not only spoke good English, but who was a very knowledgeable guide and he gave us a perfect tour of Lisbon and the surrounding areas, a tour that we will not forget. The part that stayed vividly on my mind was when our guide offered to take us to a beautiful and romantic restaurant, located on the most western point of Europe, built on the top of huge rocks in a fantastic beach, surrounded by thousands of noisy seagulls and over looking that stormy Atlantic Ocean. The food was just the way I remember it in my old country, especially the sea food, the way it smelled, the way they cooked it, and the way they cleaned it and presented it at the table; "I am HOME now", I whispered to myself (as I was looking at the whole, grilled fish, about twelve inches long, presented to us at the table on this fabulous restaurant). I feel that I left my heart in Lisbon.

As a special treat for me, it was Marta Alicia's idea for us to take a ride to Porto, where we celebrated my seventy seventh birthday.

From Lisbon we flew to Miami and then came home to live a normal and happy life, going back to reality, while carrying with us all those beautiful memories, not only of the various parts of the world we had a chance to visit, but also of those pleasurable times we spent at the ship with all the friends we made during those fifty five days of cruising. The invasion of American and Allied troops in Iraq was now in full force and rightly or wrongly, it produced an excitement with everyone who happened to care a great deal about the freedom of all the people around the world. For my part, I prefer that, only the future events and the historical outcome of this extremely complex situation will be the judge, and I don't believe that anyone with a fair mind can decide right now, what, if any, would be the benefits of the free world, from attacking Iraq.

My attention now is turned mostly to the situation with my son Steve, which has become very worrisome. Based on many contacts with him in the months ahead, I came to realize that something was seriously wrong in his life. He constantly demonstrated an unhappy picture with his new family and he seemed unable to come up with some sort of solution. He seemed like he did not want to continue what he had gotten involved with, but at the same time, he felt too weak to make any changes. He made a special effort, however, to come and visit us with his two children, Nicholas and Felicia, around June of 2003. They spent one week with us and we had a good visit with them, especially with the children, who, I must say, seemed to adore Marta Alicia and me. But for the first time in my life, I noticed something entirely different about Steve. His whole attitude had changed, his enthusiastic personality, his smile, his energy and so on, were all gone. As a matter of fact, Marta Alicia and I noted something very disturbing. We had purchased some beer for him, (I always remembered him liking a beer or two), but to our surprise, he seemed to have way too much of it, and that became very scary. He did not seem to be intoxicated however, but rather withdrawn. I spent some time alone with him trying to find out how he was doing with his situation and how he was coping with his problems with his marriage to Michelle and the only thing I received from him was, "Dad I am managing, and the most important thing for me is to see you, and to know how well you are, and that you managed to have such a good life with 'MOMMA'. You were always a good father to me, the best father in the world."

Although his words sounded quite good, I somehow sensed that, deep down; there was something to be very concerned about.

I remember very clearly that as we said goodbye at the airport I had some very strange feeling about Steve's future. I hugged him very hard, and so did he, with tears in our eyes.

But from that day on I made an extra effort to stay in closer contact with him and as I was doing that I found out some very disturbing issues.

It was one evening that I had to get some details from Steve, and when I called, Michelle answered the phone and I immediately received the information that I was suspecting for some time. It was obvious that, from the way she was talking, she was intoxicated, and after a small chat with her, she confessed to me something that I hoped I would never hear. "Let me tell you Harry", she started, "maybe you don't know it, but Steve and I are alcoholics, and that is the reason we are having all these problems. We have tried to get some help, but it does not seem to work. We love each other but we can not continue living together this way, and we don't know how to do this." Well, I don't know if I was in shock or I was hearing something that I suspected a long time ago, and it was now confirmed, or both.I don't have any way to explain how I felt from that point on. I never confronted Steve about that revelation of his alcoholism. All I could do was to show him that I would be there for him for any decision he would make, but I explained to him my concern about the problems with alcohol. I did however, remind him of the discussion we had when he was visiting us here in Naples. Most specifically was the fact that I had proposed to him that the next time I would visit them in California, that all four of us, John, Steve, Eric and I would go to visit their mother's grave, and he seemed to like the idea very much.Now that I look back, almost two years later, I must admit that I have some regrets for not paying closer attention to the signals I was receiving from both, Steve and Michelle. For the life of me, I could not believe that Steve, having gone through a first hand experience with his poor mother, (having so many problems, and going through hell with her alcoholic life style), would not be able to have developed a good vision and to see how toxic a loving relationship would turn out to be, if one does not have the emotional strength to distance himself from that harmful element. But for whatever reason, Steve seemed to be the only victim of a bad family environment and the only one to lose his spirit and energy, to turn away from such a self-distracting habit. But, nevertheless, in spite of all my anxious and concerned efforts, the tragic event that followed brought me to a point of almost total loss.

# CHAPTER 18 – Tragedy Struck Me

It was now about seven thirty in the evening on April 9, 2004. Marta Alicia was about to finish preparing dinner, she was cooking fish, being what it was, a Greek Holy Friday, during Easter season. I was watching the evening news, when the phone rang. John was on the line and with a trembling voice, which I could hardly hear, he said, "Dad I have some terrible, very terrible news, it is about Steve". "What happened" I asked. "Dad ….. He killed himself, he actually HANGED himself, Dad……….." At the beginning, I couldn't respond, except to say: "No, No, No" with pain in my voice. Marta Alicia heard my reaction and started to shout "What happened? What is going on?" When I told her that Steve was gone, her response was: "No it can't be, it can't be." She felt the need to have some emotional support and called a number of close friends and neighbors, so they could come and give us some comfort. That alone helped to put myself together.

In a couple of days we were on our way to California for what was a prearranged service for Steve. On my way there, the whole life of Steve and me started to unfold; from the beginning, when he was born, until the day John phoned with the bad news. I started thinking how can this be possible? What kind of tragedy can a father go through, harder than that, not only the event but the way it came about? Like a motion picture I was seeing him grow up from the time he was crawling to the time he was on his skis, to the time he was riding his first motorcycle, to the time he was driving his first car, to the time he was graduating from high school, to the time he was marrying Pam, to the time Nicholas and Felicia were born and to the time he bought his first home! But more than that, my thoughts turned to the time of my life when I started to follow my dream, my idea that life in America was what I really needed to be happy, the country that was supposed to offer me all kinds of opportunities and a bright future! So, where did I go so WRONG? Why one of the most beautiful presents given to me, my beloved son, Steve, had to pay the ultimate price; to give up his life, only because the present society, the new world, has decayed to such a low level that many people, young and old, started to decompose, mentally and physically and find themselves in a hopeless state of affairs! Why? Yes, Why?

The service for Steve was as nice as it could possibly be, under the circumstances. I was able to put myself together and got the courage to give a small and emotional farewell speech that helped me to start putting together my train of thoughts.

Next day, as I had promised to Steve, I asked John and Eric to join me in driving to visit their mother's grave and that gave me the most strength, by asking her to (now that she is with him), to really try to love him more than ever, because he needed it now.

But what really gave me the booster I needed most, under the circumstances, was the letter Steve wrote, just before he took his own life, and here it is in some summation:

> "To my Father, please try to forgive me.
> You may think that it's the worst thing for
> a Father to outlive his son, but I feel that
> I have tried every other means to put a stop
> to my pain. I want you to know, from the

very core of my soul that you have been in
my thoughts along with Nikko and Felicia
every day of my life. Please try to understand
that the pain was too much for me to handle.
You, Marta, and my son and daughter have
given me the strength to make it as long as I have.
I want you to know that if it wasn't for you and
your love and all the terrific examples you set for
me and my brothers, our life would have been
so empty. I hold the deepest respect for you
and the love for you. My great Father, my hero!
Please try to forgive me, if you can.

"With all my love, Steve.

I must admit that if it was not for the love and support I received from my wife, Marta Alicia, and the rest of the family, I really don't know how and when I would have managed to overcome that tragic time of my life. But I have, and I feel the need to write about his influence on me and to be able to put all of this in a story book, so, somehow, somebody, somewhere, will read it and benefit from the tragic lose of a beautiful human being.

Here I am now, an eighty year old, writing the story of my life, which was full of excitement, with all kinds of unusual, unique, adventurous and tragic events, but most of all it was rooted in one fundamental element and that was LOVE. The love my parents instilled in me from the moment they gave me my first breath until now and hopefully I will carry that tradition until my last breath leaves my body.

# IN CONCLUSION –

It has become evident to me that the world of today is manifesting is that there must be a better way to interpret why we are in this sad stage of affairs. Should we be looking back in the history of all civilizations? And I believe, here lays the answer to that.

Thousands of years ago there were three world Empires, the Greek, the Roman, and the Ottoman, all of them collapsed but for different reasons. The Greeks were more concerned on spreading Arts, Science, and Culture, but no too much effort was made on economic developments and major industrializations. That very fact doomed them, and Greece became one of the poorest countries in the world, just because they believed to do good for humanity and also in feeling good by doing GOOD.

The Romans were too much concerned on conquering and controlling most of the existing world and became the most corrupt power during their Reign.

The Ottoman Empire was destroyed because the rest of the world hated them for being ruthless, killers, and the worst, "Barbaric" rulers the world had ever known.

In my opinion the modern world is facing a serious problem leading to its destruction. The "LOVE" and care for one another is almost gone and so is the family structure. Where is the family dinner around the table? Where is the "PASS THE MASHED POTATOS" type of home life style? Where is the social harmony? We lack the trust from the fellow man, a fact which is now manifested in every day life. So much fear! Now, regarding the aspect of fear, here is a typical example of what we are facing today.

A few weeks ago while visiting our grandchildren in Seattle we went to The Children's Museum of Science. There were hundreds of toddlers running around, having fun. All of a sudden, a beautiful little girl about three years old apparently thinking that I was her grandfather, ran into me and grabbed my legs. However, when she looked up and saw me, she started screaming, crying and shaking like maple leaf in a windy afternoon. Obviously, nowadays, parents instruct their children to: "DON'T TRUST OR TALK TO STRANGERS", and who could blame them? That's why kids, today, sadly, develop an instant mistrust for today's society. How tragic!

I do believe that all the good qualities of mankind, yes HUMANS, are, so ever slowly, being replaced by new TECHNOLOGICAL systems, which are trying to reach out to global contacts and relations, to the extent that the human element, the true feelings and the tenderness, which distinguishes MAN from ANIMALS, is being replaced by grossly inhuman electronic communications VEHICLES. But I sincerely believe that, if the kind of GREEK SPIRIT could possibly return and spread through out the world and produce a balanced approach, a COMPROMISE; maybe there is a chance that the whole world would benefit from it, on a permanent basis. I, however, must admit that, what I am hopping for here, is as realistic as asking the Earth to change its course and start rotating in the opposite direction, but the point I am trying to make here is that some "DRASTIC" changes in the human behavior around the world must take place TODAY, before it turns to dust.

Here is a typical example, of what I am referring to regarding the non-human technological behavior which I experienced very recently. Our computer, all of a sudden stopped working. We asked a young man to help us repair it. He looked at it for five minutes and concluded that, "This is a piece of junk". We agreed that we needed to replace it, and he did. What the most amazing thing for me was, looking at this young man, (about the same age as I was when I came in this country, about twenty seven years of age,) as I was observing the way he was trying to make the computer work, to program it, looking at the monitor in silence and in total concentration; he seemed like if he was looking at the stars in a clear night, trying to find out various galaxies and comets, or something like "out in space", in a complete absorption, totally emotionless, and cold, almost the type of behavior one would expect from a robot. He did fix it, however, and it worked very well. We paid him and he was on his way, he disappeared almost silently.

That was so scary, and it made me believe that the modern technological ADVANCES tend to eliminate the NOBLE human contacts and replace them with cold, indifferent, machine-like behavior.

I hope and pray that some part of my ideas and concerns, which I have expressed here, in my story book, regarding social needs, such as. LOVE, trust, and true care for the fellow human being, will find some fertile ground in today's world terrain and spread seeds for the use of improving, somehow, the present way of life of some people.

*******

# About the Author

Harry Mourelatos was born and raised in Athens Greece. When he was twenty seven he decided to leave behind his loving family and travel to America to find future and opportunity. Although he came alone he was able to create a "Mourelatos Clan" to the tune of forty two members. He wrote his first and only book in memory of his beloved son Steve.